THE NEW BUFFALO

Minneapolis

First Edition December 2025

The New Buffalo: Leonard Prescott and the Origins of Indian Gaming.

10 9 8 7 6 5 4 3 2 1

ISBN: 978-1-962834-63-6

Cover and book design by Gary Lindberg

THE NEW BUFFALO

LEONARD PRESCOTT AND THE ORIGINS OF INDIAN GAMING

GARY LINDBERG

Minneapolis

Also by Gary Lindberg

FICTION

The Shekinah Legacy

Sons of Zadok

The Unspoken

The Mount

Deeper and Deeper

Ollie's Cloud

John Ross

NONFICTION

Letters from Elvis

Brando On Elvis

The Roots of Elvis

The Soul of Humanity

Humanity Coming of Age

Seeing God in Many Mirrors

The Power of Positive Handwriting

An Improbable Series of Risky Events

Table of Contents

Introduction 1

The New Buffalo 7

PART 1: NEWCOMERS 11

The Feast and the Fracture 13

After the Ashes 31

The Emergence of the New Buffalo 41

PART 2: LEONARD 55

The Boy Who Climbed the Cottonwood 57

Family Life On the Reservation 61

The Melting Pot 69

Stark Realities 75

Unexpected Doors 91

Integrity as Survival 107

A Return to Spirit 121

Bingo 127

Beginning of a Feud 133

The Fall of a Chairman 141

PART 3: CHAIRMAN LEONARD PRESCOTT 155

The Aftermath 157

To Washington and Beyond 173

Sparks in Silicon – Video Games of Chance 183

The $8.8 Million Loan 191

The Compacts of a Lifetime 209
Lines of Blood and Lines of Power 219
The Dismantling of Little Six 237
The Battle Over Adoptees 249
The Rise and Missteps of Foxwoods 261
The Echo of Little Crow 267

Acknowledgements 273
About the Author 275

Introduction

I am not an Indian. That simple fact will prompt some readers to wonder what right I have to tell this story about Tribal gaming—one braided from the histories, sorrows, and triumphs of Native Nations. I have asked myself that same question throughout this project. My answer is twofold. First, the origin of modern Tribal gaming is not just a Native story; it is an American story—legal, political, economic, spiritual—and it touches every jurisdiction from federal courts to county boards, from reservation councils to state capitols. Second, this book's central figures, events, and controversies virtually require an objective, third-party narrator—someone outside the family and factional lines—to assemble the record, listen carefully to the people who lived it, and present it without fear or favor.

This is a complex narrative. It spans the long arc from treaty promises between the US government and Native American tribes and dispossession, to the assertion of sovereignty through economic self-determination. It traverses Supreme Court holdings and Department of the Interior memos, enrollment rolls and constitutional clauses. It moves through bingo halls that became engines of renewal and through council chambers where a single vote could turn prosperity into peril. It is also intimate—a life story shaped by childhood neighborhoods, by losses endured and disciplines learned, by moments of vision that arrived like lightning and had to be carried, with both hands, into the work of governance.

Some of the boxes of correspondence, memos, governmental actions and other records regarding Indian gaming and Shakopee Mdewakanton Sioux Community affairs.

At the center stands Leonard Prescott. His path—sometimes halting, often courageous—threads through the formative years of the Shakopee Mdewakanton Sioux Community's modern era and through the national push that culminated in the Indian Gaming Regulatory Act. In Leonard's telling, the fight for gaming was never simply about money. It was about the conditions that make self-government real: defining a citizenry; securing land; building institutions that are sturdy enough to withstand pressure from within and without; and insisting that federal trustees meet their duties while respecting the inherent sovereignty of Native Nations. His life intersected family loyalties and factional politics, corporate design and cultural inheritance, courtrooms and backrooms. In the pages that follow, you will see how those intersections forged both opportunity and conflict.

If your prior mental picture of Indian gaming is a gleaming casino and a tidy revenue line, this book asks you to widen the frame. The story is fraught with episodes of government overreach and neglect; there are competing interpretations of constitutions and membership criteria; there are painful disputes over adoptions and enrollments; there are bruising leadership contests and accusations that still sting. There are also acts of prudence and foresight: building corporate structures to protect assets from political swings; separating business operations from legislative authority; crafting regulatory systems that could satisfy skeptical partners; and carrying the hard, unglamorous work of governance day after day.

A word about method. The chapters that follow draw on interviews and personal papers, community records, federal and Tribal legal documents, public reporting, and the testimony of people who were there. I have tried to render their words faithfully and to distinguish recollection from documentary fact where the distinction matters. When the sources conflict, I identify the fault lines and explain why I have rendered the scene as I do. Where legal issues arise, I translate the jargon and show how a clause or ruling shaped real human lives. Where memory carries pain, I try to handle it with care.

Because questions of identity and belonging are central to this story, I address them directly. In many Native communities, debates over membership—lineal descent, blood quantum, adoption—are not abstractions; they determine who has a voice, who holds land assignments, who votes, who benefits, and who decides. These are constitutional matters, but they are also matters of kinship and dignity. The book follows how these questions played out in one community under pressure and how those pressures intersected with federal oversight, state relations, and the new economics of gaming.

The book operates on two levels. At ground level, there is the biography of a leader—a boy learning to read the streets of Saint Paul; a young man absorbing lessons about fairness the hard way; a chairman trying to cool tempers while pushing institutions forward; an advocate riding the shuttle to Washington, stitching together coalitions and language precise enough to stand in federal law. At the wider level, there is the transformation of Indian Country's economic landscape—court decisions that opened doors; compacts that harnessed or hindered momentum; technologies that changed the very nature of games; and the often-misunderstood relationship between sovereignty and regulation.

Readers will encounter names that elicit pride in some quarters and anger in others. You will see how old disagreements about treaties and trusteeship echoed in late-twentieth-century fights over ordinances and enrollment lists. You will see how personality and principle collided and how even justified outrage had to be channeled into draft language, vote counts, and compliance systems if anything durable was going to be built. You will see, too, how success bred new responsibilities: to elders and children, to culture and language, to neighbors and employees, to the land itself.

If you are Native and come to these pages wary of yet another outsider's account, I ask only this: Judge the work on its own merits, not on prior prejudices. Judge it by whether it quotes accurately, sets scenes fairly, and keeps returning to first principles—sovereignty, consent, accountability, and care for the People. If you are not Native and come as a curious citizen or policymaker, I invite you to bring an open mind and not to let this history complicate any easy caricatures, favorable or hostile, that you may have absorbed.

Finally, a note about tone. This is not a prosecution brief, nor is it a press release. It is a report of what happened as best as it can be told with respect for those who carried the burdens and made the calls in real time. Where the record is clear, I say so. Where it is contested, I show you the contest. Where private grief touched public duty, I try to honor both.

Tribal gaming did not descend fully formed from a single court case, a single leader, or a single meeting. It emerged from decades of legal argument, political negotiation, technological change, and community resolve. It rose from councils where people spoke sharply and then showed up again the next night. It rose from a conviction—tested, battered, but not extinguished—that Native Nations could shape their own futures.

Lastly, a word about language. I have been asked about the use of the word "buffalo" throughout these pages since the animal referred to is now known as the American bison. Native people use the word "buffalo" for the American bison because early English and French explorers applied their familiar European term *buffalo / bouef* to the huge plains animals they encountered. The name stuck in trade language, treaty language, and daily speech, and Native nations adopted it because it entered the shared vocabulary long before "bison" became the scientific term. In Native usage, "buffalo" isn't a misnomer—it carries cultural, spiritual, and historical meaning tied to the animal that sustained their societies for thousands of years.

If this book succeeds, it will be because the people who lived this history allowed me to sit at their tables, to ask impertinent questions, and to carry their words forward with care. I thank them. And I ask you, the reader, to step into the story with patience and humility. There is much here to learn and, more importantly, much here to meet with a clear eye and an open heart.

The New Buffalo

In the quiet twilight between dreaming and awakening, a venerable buffalo hunter opened his eyes to find himself walking upon strange, hard paths beneath unfamiliar skies. The hunter, whose veins flowed with the wisdom of the old ceremonies, felt his heart tighten with sorrow, for the avenue he walked was not of the grasslands, nor of sacred earth, but Franklin Avenue in Minneapolis, a place haunted by echoes of his People's grief. Here, shadows filled with suffering whispered from doorways, telling stories of broken homes, tormented elders, lost youth, and dreams stolen by the bitter claws of despair.

Distressed yet resolute, he returned to his small room—a hollow place, devoid of the songs of the wind or the heartbeat of the earth. Kneeling, he began to chant and pray, his voice carrying to the Grandfathers who watch from the farthest stars.

"Grandfathers," he called, "you promised us a day of strength and renewal. When will my People rise again?"

From the silent expanse of the spirit world came their gentle whisper, "Patience, warrior. Your answer is near."

Dawn awakened the buffalo hunter with an insistent whisper guiding him to an open field untouched by despair, luminous in the morning sun. And there stood a Great White Buffalo, majestic and shimmering like starlight made flesh. Tears of gratitude streamed down the hunter's face as he knelt, humbled before this vision. "Grandfathers," he breathed, "you have heard me. Here is the beast whose spirit and body can restore my People."

But the White Buffalo was elusive, swift as lightning, wise as the wind. The buffalo hunter's arrows sailed through air but touched no flesh; every trap dissolved like mist. The hunter's heart grew heavy with failure, and so he prayed once more. "Grandfathers, grant me the means to capture this blessing, to carry him home to those who hunger."

Again the Grandfathers counseled patience, promising guidance. With the next sunrise came a curious gift of strange clothing unlike anything he had ever worn—a coat, pants, shirt, and tie, the garments of the very people who had taken so much from his People. Hesitant yet obedient, he dressed himself. Awkwardness gave way to surprise. The clothes fit well, though they felt like wearing borrowed skin.

When the hunter walked forth in this disguise, the world around him shifted. A White man who once spat upon his shadow now greeted him with cautious respect. With renewed confidence, the hunter returned to the field, and there the White Buffalo awaited, calm and watchful. This time, as he moved, the Buffalo mirrored him, step for step, until both stood in quiet communion at the field's heart.

"Brother Buffalo," the hunter spoke softly, his words trembling with truth, "once your kind filled this land. Then the invaders came, taking everything until we knew only hunger and grief. Now, poverty, sickness and despair fill our days."

The Buffalo listened patiently, and after a long silence, replied, "Brother human, I know your pain. I have returned to offer myself to your People, that they may regain what was lost."

With solemn reverence, the buffalo hunter brought the gift home. As the people feasted, they regained their strength. Clothed in the buffalo's hide, they were warmed. Holding the sacred bones, they remembered their ancient prayers, and hope ignited within them once more.

And across many lands, the hunter saw more White Buffalo appearing, sacred yet fragile. He warned the chiefs, who sought the counsel of the Grandfathers. The wise spirits spoke urgently, "Guard this Buffalo carefully, for it is born of two worlds—the red and the white. The old threat still lingers. Protect your Buffalo, or the strangers will again seize your blessing."

Thus began a new pursuit, the quest to create their own Buffalo, a creature resilient and strong—born not of chance, but of wisdom, courage and unity, forever ensuring that their People's pride, strength, and sustenance would never again vanish from the earth.

As the seasons turned, the vision of the White Buffalo transformed into a powerful new spirit. Rising like dawn across Tribal lands, it took a new form—a modern Buffalo crafted from ingenuity, determination, and sovereignty. Tribal gaming became this new Buffalo, offering nourishment and prosperity to communities once trapped in shadows. Casinos and resorts blossomed like meadows after rain, reviving pride, self-reliance, and cultural renewal. This new Buffalo was a bridge between worlds, a testament to resilience, empowering the People not merely to survive, but to thrive, restoring dignity and fulfilling the ancient prophecy in ways the buffalo hunter had never imagined.

PART 1:
NEWCOMERS

The Feast and the Fracture

Before there were borders, before there were maps, before the name "America" even echoed across the oceans, this land was already home to Nations. Not just villages, and certainly not savages, but sovereign Nations, each with its own language, beliefs, laws, and leaders. The Lakota knew the stars differently than the Haudenosaunee. The Choctaw sang their prayers with different drums than the Salish. From the snow-swept woodlands of the Abenaki to the sun-scorched mesas of the Hopi, this continent was as varied as Europe itself. And like Europe, its Nations sometimes traded, sometimes allied—and sometimes went to war.

Into this great interwoven fabric of peoples came the newcomers.

They arrived by sail, their wooden hulls groaning with the weight of desperation and the promise of dominion. The ones who landed in what would become Plymouth were not the first, nor would they be the last. But they came with a particular story—of a failed harvest, a harsh winter, and a nearly broken spirit. Of all the truths and half-truths handed down through the generations, this remains certain: Without help, the Pilgrims would not have survived.

It was the Wampanoag who helped them—Massasoit, the sachem of a powerful confederation of tribes, who extended an arm not of conquest, but of cautious alliance. His People had been ravaged by disease brought by earlier European explorers, losing entire villages in a matter of moons. The Wampanoag were in need of allies as much as the Pilgrims were in need of food.

So in 1621, after the harvest, there was a feast.

Not the solemn, quaint dinner painted by schoolbooks and cranberry sauce advertisements, but a three-day gathering of cultures and survival. Wildfowl, venison, squash, and corn roasted over open fires. Games were played. Words were exchanged. Tobacco passed from hand to hand, spirit to spirit. Two peoples sat side by side—wary, different, but sharing.

And for a moment, it worked.

But moments, like seasons, pass.

The land—the endless, fertile land—was the first point of tension. To the Pilgrims and those who came after, land was property, a thing to be claimed, fenced, and willed to sons. To the Wampanoag and most Indigenous Nations, land was sacred, alive, not owned but lived with. When they "sold" land, it was often in the spirit of shared use, not relinquishment. But the settlers did not understand—or chose not to.

As more ships arrived and colonies grew, the balance shifted. What had once been mutual dependence became a one-sided hunger. Forests fell. Villages vanished. Treaties were made, then broken. The Pilgrims' children no longer saw the Wampanoag as partners, but as obstacles.

It did not take long for the feast to sour.

At first, it was the land. There was always more of it—green, rolling, unfenced. In the eyes of the newcomers, it was abundant and unused—wasteful, even. They looked upon the meadows, forests, and winding rivers as untouched riches waiting to be claimed. In their old world, land was property. A man might be poor, but with land, he could rise. With land, he could plant. With land, he could own his future.

But for the Native Nations, the land was not theirs to own. It was sacred. It breathed. It had spirit. A river did not belong to the People; the People belonged to the river. It was not "property" but a relative—grandmother, brother, child. The idea of selling land was foreign, even absurd. And when they did make agreements, they were rooted in relationships, shared use, and obligations of respect—not in deeds and forever rights of ownership.

This was the first misunderstanding, or perhaps the first willful ignorance.

The English settlers—then the Dutch, the Swedes, and eventually the Americans—began to draw lines, not in conversation but in ink. They put fences around invisible borders and called them theirs. They planted flags and wrote titles, carving up a living land into paper parcels.

When the absurdly named "Indians" resisted, settlers saw them as dangerous obstacles. Savages. When Indians honored spiritual obligations over contracts, they were labeled untrustworthy. When they defended their homes, they were called violent. When they tried to hold on to the treaties they had made in good faith, they were accused of standing in the way of progress.

And so, little by little, the feast gave way to suspicion. Suspicion to resentment. Resentment to betrayal.

The first full betrayals came clothed in promises.

Pequot and the Pattern of Fire

In 1637, barely a generation after the so-called First Thanksgiving, the English colonies turned on the Pequot People of what is now Connecticut. Tensions over land and trade had grown. A colonial fur trader was killed—allegedly by Pequot. The English response was brutal.

The English surrounded a Pequot village near the Mystic River at dawn. Men, women, and children were burned alive as their longhouse walls became walls of fire. Those who fled were cut down. Hundreds died within hours. Those not killed were sold into slavery—some to the Caribbean, others to rival tribes enlisted by the English. The war ended with the near erasure of the Pequot as a political entity.

A message had been sent—Indigenous diplomacy would be met with English dominion.

Still, many Tribal Nations tried to avoid the same fate. Some chose accommodation. Others withdrew deeper into their homelands. But peace was always temporary.

The Walking Purchase and the Art of the Lie

The Lenape People—often called the Delaware by Europeans—once lived throughout Pennsylvania and New Jersey, with deep spiritual ties to the land and a long tradition of negotiating in good faith. In 1737, they were betrayed by a particularly egregious manipulation—the so-called Walking Purchase.

Colonial authorities produced a suspiciously convenient "deed" that claimed the Lenape had promised to sell as much land as a man could walk in a day and a half. But instead of a negotiated pace, the colonists employed trained runners and cleared a path to maximize distance. In less than two days, they claimed over a million acres of Lenape land.

When the Lenape protested, they were ignored. When they resisted, they were labeled hostile. Many were pushed west, into unfamiliar territory already occupied by other Nations. Violence between tribes followed, often encouraged or exploited by colonial powers.

These betrayals created a new reality. Indians learned that even written treaties, signed in public with pomp and ceremony, were tools of deceit. The settlers made agreements not to uphold them, but to momentarily pacify resistance. The ink was barely dry before the knives came out.

The Covenant Fractures

Throughout the 18th century, Indigenous Nations engaged in a complex dance of diplomacy, especially during the French and Indian War. Different tribes aligned with French or British forces hoping to preserve their homelands or gain advantage against rival Indian Nations. This era—like Europe's own centuries of war—was not simple, not romantic, and certainly not united.

The idea of a monolithic "Indian" identity had never existed. Tribes fought each other, made alliances, betrayed one another, and navigated politics with as much cunning as any European state. But they all shared one common threat—the creeping, endless tide of immigrant expansion.

After Britain's victory in 1763, Indian hopes for protection under French alliances vanished. Pontiac's Rebellion—a pan-Indian uprising—sought to push back against British forts and policies. Though it had early success, it was brutally crushed. British authorities responded by declaring the Proclamation Line of 1763, ostensibly protecting Native lands west of the Appalachians.

It was a lie in slow motion.

Settlers ignored the line. Colonial governments encouraged migration. The British, facing rebellion in their own colonies, turned a blind eye.

The Birth of a Nation, the Death of a Promise

When the American Revolution erupted, Indian Nations were forced into impossible choices. Some allied with the British, hoping they would restrain colonial land theft. Others tried to remain neutral. A few sided with the revolutionaries. None would be spared.

After the Revolution, the new United States of America treated all Indian alliances as acts of war. The British, in their treaty with

America, ceded Indian lands they didn't own to the new country, handing over the Ohio Valley and the Great Lakes territories like goods in a ledger.

No Indian Nation was even consulted.

The United States quickly set to claiming and selling this land. Treaties were signed with tribes one day and broken the next. In 1790, the US passed the Indian Trade and Intercourse Act to regulate commerce with tribes and promise fairness. But settlers continued to pour into Native lands, often protected by militias or emboldened by official neglect.

Tribes that resisted were attacked. Tribes that signed treaties saw their lands steadily shrink. They were callously told to "civilize"—to become farmers, Christians, and Americans—or be removed.

And when persuasion failed, the sword followed.

Removal, Resettlement, and the Crumbling Middle Ground

By the dawn of the 19th century, the United States had declared its ambition without apology—expansion, unbroken from coast to coast. What had once been settlements hugging the Atlantic became a national appetite stretching westward—an appetite insatiable and cloaked in divine justification. "Manifest Destiny," they called it. A God-given right to conquer and civilize the wilderness. But the so-called wilderness was not empty. Never had been. It was homeland—populated, named, remembered.

To feed this ambition, the government set its hand to the systematic removal of Indigenous Nations. The Indian Removal Act was passed in 1830. It was championed by President Andrew Jackson, whose personal hatred of Native resistance had been forged in military campaigns against the Creeks and Seminoles. This Act codified displacement as national policy and granted the president authority to negotiate land exchanges with tribes to forcibly relocate them west of the Mississippi. Though couched in terms of negotiation, the law effectively nullified Tribal sovereignty. Treaties became tools of coercion, and any refusal to cede land could be met with military action. Treaties—often signed by Indian chiefs under duress or deception—were used to justify forced marches, broken communities, and untold death.

Then the federal government under President Jackson ignored settled law in Worcester v. Georgia (1832), in which the Supreme Court had ruled that state laws had no authority on Tribal land. Jackson responded to the decision with defiance, allegedly stating, "[Chief Justice] John Marshall has made his decision. Now let him enforce it."

Orchestrated Exile

The "Trail of Tears" became the most infamous example of the policy of displacement. The Cherokee, who had embraced European-style farming, adopted a written constitution, and even printed a bilingual newspaper, were nonetheless herded at bayonet point from Georgia to present-day Oklahoma. Thousands died from cold, hunger, and disease. But the Cherokee were not alone. The Choctaw, Chickasaw, Creek, and Seminole suffered similar fates.

While the Trail of Tears is often told as a Southeastern story, removal policies eventually reached nearly every Tribal region in the continental United States. In the decades that followed, the Diné (Navajo) were marched three hundred miles in 1864 in the Long Walk to Bosque Redondo, where they were confined under brutal conditions. The Nez Perce, led by Chief Joseph, fled over a thousand miles from Oregon in a desperate bid for freedom, only to be captured forty miles from the Canadian border. Despite prior treaty guarantees, the Lakota Sioux were herded onto reservations after losing the Black Hills and then were massacred at Wounded Knee in 1890.

These were not just military actions. They were economic ones as well. The fertile land from which southern tribes were driven was prime for cotton plantations and the expanding system of Black slavery. In this way, Indian removal became the twin sibling of slavery—both systems serving White wealth, both justified by racial superiority, both built on dispossession and violence.

Yet even as these removals scarred the Southeast, a different pressure began to build in the Upper Midwest, where the Dakota, Ojibwe, Ho-Chunk and other Nations still lived along the rivers, lakes, and forestlands.

Minnesota—then part of a larger frontier—was still a place where cultures met uneasily. The Dakota, also known as the Eastern Sioux, had long lived in the region where they hunted, farmed and traded. Their villages stretched along the Minnesota and Mississippi rivers, and their lives were rooted in deep seasonal rhythms.

The Dakota were not strangers to change. For decades, they had traded with French, British, and later American fur companies. They had adapted, negotiated, and navigated shifting relationships. This borderland had once been a middle ground, where Native diplomacy could hold space with colonial needs. But as the American presence thickened into permanence, that space collapsed.

More settlers arrived. More land was wanted. And with each treaty, the Dakota were pushed farther from their traditional ways.

The Treaties of 1837 and 1851

In 1837, a treaty between the US government and the Dakota promised annuity payments, goods, and services in exchange for ceding vast tracts of land east of the Mississippi. But almost immediately, promises were broken. Payments were late or skimmed off by corrupt traders. Supplies were poor in quality, and government agents treated Indian leaders with contempt.

Still, the Dakota endured. They fished the rivers, gathered wild rice and hunted game in the forests. They held to their ceremonies and tried to protect what remained.

But the settler hunger for land never abated.

By 1851, the Treaty of Traverse des Sioux and the Treaty of Mendota stripped the Dakota of nearly all their remaining territory in southern Minnesota. In exchange, they were promised $1.4 million, much of which was eventually diverted to fur traders and bureaucrats. The treaties also created a small reservation along the Minnesota River, where the Dakota were to be confined.

The logic of the treaties was simple—take the land, confine the People, offer them a pittance to survive, and strip them of every mechanism of self-sufficiency.

Within a few years, the Dakota were dependent on government annuities and food deliveries that came late, if at all. Their buffalo hunts had been curtailed. Their sacred rhythms had been broken. And the new economy—the *settler* economy—left no room for them.

Meanwhile, settler farms and towns grew fat on the land that had once been theirs.

"Let Them Eat Grass"

By the summer of 1862, the Dakota were starving.

That June, heavy rains and poor crop yields left the reservation in crisis. Hunting had failed as game had grown scarce. The federal annuity payments promised by treaty—money and supplies crucial for survival—had not arrived.

When Dakota leaders pleaded for food on credit, they were dismissed. Traders like Andrew Myrick, who had grown wealthy off government contracts, reportedly sneered, "Let them eat grass or their own dung." Myrick supplied goods to the Dakota—often on credit—and was deeply entangled in the "traders' claims" system, whereby US annuity payments to the Dakota were frequently intercepted to repay alleged and often fraudulent Tribal debts.

Myrick's spiteful statement would echo as children went hungry, elders died quietly in their lodges, and proud hunters were reduced to begging. The Dakota had been pressed too far, and the federal government, distracted by the Civil War, offered little notice.

But Dakota anger had been growing—not just for weeks, but for generations. Younger Dakota men, many of whom had never signed the treaties, saw the starvation of their families as a final humiliation. Elders spoke of broken promises and sacred responsibilities. Warriors remembered the old ways. Among them, a new fire took hold.

Some tried to counsel peace, fearing the full weight of the US military. But others believed they had nothing left to lose. If death was coming, it would not come quietly.

On August 17, 1862, four young Dakota men, hunting near Acton Township, encountered a settler family. What began as a tense encounter quickly turned deadly. Five settlers were killed. The violence, like a struck match, lit the prairie.

That night, Dakota leaders debated. Should they surrender the killers and seek calm, or take this moment to rise against their oppressors?

Led by Little Crow, a respected but cautious chief, the Dakota made their choice—it would be war.

The Prairie Burns—The US-Dakota War of 1862

On the morning of August 18, 1862, the prairie held its breath.

At dawn, Dakota warriors struck the Lower Sioux Agency in the town of Morton—a government outpost meant to distribute annuity goods but often remembered more for the corruption and contempt its buildings housed. Storehouses were set ablaze. Traders and government agents were killed. Among them was the despised Andrew Myrick, whose mutilated body was later found with his mouth stuffed full of grass—a grim echo of his taunt, now made prophecy.

The Dakota moved swiftly. They targeted isolated farms and homesteads, striking before word of the attack could spread. Panic rippled across the Minnesota River Valley. Settler families fled eastward, many on foot, leaving behind crops, tools and homes. Towns like New Ulm and Hutchinson hastily erected barricades. Militia units were formed from volunteers, and Civil War veterans rushed from southern garrisons.

Little Crow, the reluctant leader turned wartime general, tried to impose discipline among his warriors. He saw this not as a raid but as a chance to reclaim sovereignty, to force the US government to take seriously the broken treaties and starvation it had inflicted. Yet even he could not fully control the chaos of war. Some Dakota, fueled by vengeance and hunger, took captives—mostly women and children. Others exacted revenge for decades of degradation, their fury sharpened by grief.

To many settlers, it was a bloodbath. To the Dakota, it was an uprising long in the making.

A War on Two Fronts

News of the uprising reached Saint Paul within days. The timing could not have been worse for the Union. The Civil War was at its height, and most regular troops were away fighting Confederate forces. Still, Governor Alexander Ramsey responded quickly. He appointed Colonel Henry Sibley, a former fur trader and Minnesota's first governor, to lead a hastily assembled force to suppress the Dakota.

Sibley's advance was slow. Supply lines were stretched, and many of his men lacked training. Meanwhile, the Dakota pushed north and east, attacking Fort Ridgely and laying siege to New Ulm. Both attacks failed to produce decisive victories, but they spread fear through the White population, causing mass evacuations and near hysteria across Minnesota.

Among the Dakota, there were divisions. Not all supported the war. Some bands—especially among the Sisseton and Wahpeton—refused to join the fighting. Others actively protected settler families or acted as intermediaries. The war was never a unanimous Tribal action but a splintered, desperate surge from those most affected by hunger and betrayal.

Still, Little Crow pressed on, even as the tide began to turn.

By late September, Sibley's reinforced army clashed with Dakota warriors at the Battle of Wood Lake. It was a decisive defeat for Little Crow's forces. The Dakota fled westward, while hundreds of others—many of whom had not fought—sought surrender or refuge.

The war was effectively over in six weeks. But its consequences were just beginning.

Trials Without Justice

In the aftermath, over two thousand Dakota men, women and children surrendered or were captured. The US government, eager for retribution, began military trials—swift, chaotic tribunals that sometimes lasted mere minutes. Witnesses were often absent. Translations were poor or nonexistent. Many Indian defendants did not understand the charges against them.

In the end, over three hundred Dakota men were sentenced to death.

President Abraham Lincoln, under pressure from political allies and advisors, reviewed the cases personally. After days of agonizing scrutiny, he commuted most of the sentences, insisting that only thirty-eight executions be carried out—those accused of the most direct and brutal civilian killings.

Still, this marked the largest mass execution in US history.

On December 26, 1862, the thirty-eight Dakota men were hanged in Mankato, Minnesota, as a crowd of thousands gathered to watch. Drums did not beat. No songs rose to the sky. Just silence—and then the drop.

In the weeks that followed, Dakota families—many of whom had not taken part in the war—were marched to Fort Snelling, where they were held in a concentration camp beneath the bluffs. Disease and cold took dozens of lives through the bitter winter. Eventually, survivors were forcibly removed to reservations in Dakota Territory or Nebraska. Their homeland—Minnesota—was declared off-limits. The name "Dakota" became synonymous with savagery. Bounties were placed on those who escaped. Sacred objects were stolen or destroyed.

Shadows of Exile

The hangings in Mankato were not the end. They were the beginning of a longer death—a slower, quieter erasure that did not come by musket or rope, but by starvation, silence, and distance. When the final rope snapped beneath the thirty-eight Dakota men, the government's revenge was only half-finished. The survivors—the elders who had wept, the women who had sung over graves, the children who did not yet understand what had happened—were gathered and marched at gunpoint to Fort Snelling.

It was winter. The river had begun to freeze in thick, grey plates, and the wind howled down the bluffs like a chorus of mourning spirits. They walked in single file, blankets wrapped too thin around their shoulders. Some fell. Some did not rise again. A few clutched small bundles: bits of cornmeal, a pipe, a braid of sweetgrass hastily hidden in their clothing. Most carried nothing. What they had left behind was everything.

The camp at Fort Snelling was not a refuge. It was a prison. Surrounded by wooden palisades and White guards with cold eyes, the Dakota families were crammed into filthy quarters on the frozen flats below the fort—between the rivers, where the ground oozed cold mud and death hung in the air like breath turned to frost. Dysentery spread. So did measles. Babies died in silence, swaddled in mothers' shawls. Elders, unaccustomed to such cruelty from the elements, folded into themselves and passed without ceremony.

But even there, in the dirt and the snow, the songs did not die.

At night, when the guards turned their backs or drank themselves to sleep, soft voices rose in the dark. A grandfather whispered a prayer to the sky. A woman pressed a lullaby into her child's ear, shaping the syllables in Dakota, even as she had been told not to. And in those fragile words, the old world survived. Not as geography, but as memory. Not as place, but as heartbeat.

Spring brought no freedom—only relocation.

The government loaded the survivors onto steamboats and wagons and sent them south and west, away from their ancestral lands. The place where their grandfathers had hunted, where the rivers had taught them to fish and the prairie grasses had whispered to the children—that place was declared forbidden. Minnesota had washed its hands. The Dakota were now "other," cast out like plague-bearers from a Nation with no more room for their stories.

Some were sent to a narrow strip of reservation land near Crow Creek in present-day South Dakota. It was barren, harsh, and ill-suited for farming. Within the first year, hundreds died from starvation and disease. Others were later sent farther south to Nebraska. There, too, the soil was unfamiliar, and the government rations came late or not at all. Each time they were told this was a final solution. Each time, it was just another place to be forgotten.

They were not alone. Other Nations—Ho-Chunk, Ponca, Iowa, Sac and Fox—also found themselves displaced, sometimes layered atop one another on increasingly narrow pieces of land. What had once been a continent of many nations was now a map of shrinking islands, where entire cultures were confined like smoke in jars.

The US–Dakota War marked a turning point not only in Minnesota but across the United States. It ended, decisively, the illusion that Indians and White settlers could coexist under the framework of the treaties as they had been written. It exposed the moral bankruptcy of US Indian policy, a system built on paper promises and real starvation.

It also became a template.

In the years that followed, the removal and reservation system would accelerate. The Plains Wars would ignite. The buffalo herds would be slaughtered. The Indian boarding school system would rise. And throughout it all, the myth of the noble settler and the savage warrior would be burned into the American imagination. In countless American movies, two storylines would dominate—good-guy cops and evil robbers, and brave cowboys versus savage Indians.

State-Sponsored Cultural Genocide

Among the most despicable and damaging tactics used by the government to pacify and control Indians was the introduction of a network of boarding schools. In 1879, Captain Richard Henry Pratt founded the Carlisle Indian Industrial School in Pennsylvania. Pratt's model—later adopted across the country—was bluntly stated: "Kill the Indian, save the man." To fulfill this inhumane mission, children were taken from their homes, cut from their families, stripped of their clothing and languages, and forced into Christian discipline and vocational training.

By 1910, over sixty Indian boarding schools operated nationwide with federal funding exceeding three million dollars annually. Institutions were often militaristic, isolating, and abusive. Many Indian boarding schools in the United States were operated not directly by the federal government, but by religious organizations under contract with the Bureau of Indian Affairs (BIA). These institutions were Christian denominations, missionary societies, church-affiliated schools and private philanthropic institutions.

The largest operator of Indian boarding schools was the Catholic Church, which ran dozens of schools across the country. Catholic orders such as the Jesuits, Sisters of the Blessed Sacrament, and Franciscan friars were heavily involved. Other religious denominations also received contracts or subsidies from the BIA, including the Episcopal Church, the Methodist Church, the Presbyterian Church, the Quakers (Society of Friends), and the LDS Church (Mormons), which required students to be baptized into the LDS Church.

Research—including the US Department of the Interior's 2015 report—has confirmed widespread physical, sexual, psychological, and emotional abuse at Indian boarding schools, as well as a devastating loss of Native language, culture, tradition and family bonds.

Unfortunately for Indian families, boarding schools were not optional. Congress enacted laws obligating parents to send their children to these identity-stripping institutions. Ignoring state jurisdiction, Congress even allowed schools to arrest children. Decades of student testimony reveal children falsely labeled as orphans, widespread illness and malnutrition, and the irreparable loss of parenting skills and intergenerational education.

Each facility targeted language, spirituality, and family integrity. Traditional rites like Sun Dances and smudging were banned. Funerals and community events were curtailed. Children who resisted were punished while those who complied were stripped of identity.

Minnesota was not exempt from the boarding school strategy. Institutions included Pipestone Indian School (1887–1953), Thomas Indian School near Red Wing (circle of military camps), Red Lake Boarding School, and numerous day schools in urban centers like Minneapolis and St. Paul.

At places like Carlisle Indian Industrial School in Pennsylvania, children as young as five were taken—sometimes with parental consent extracted through pressure, sometimes by force. Their hair was cut. Their clothes were burned. They were given English names and punished for speaking their mother tongues. Boys were trained to be laborers or soldiers. Girls were taught to cook, sew, and clean in the manner of proper White housewives.

Discipline was harsh. Punishments ranged from beatings to solitary confinement. Children were buried far from home, in graves marked only with small white crosses or numbers. And yet—even there—something lived on.

Some children learned to pray in both languages. Others carved symbols into bedposts or whispered songs into their pillows. A few brave teachers or staff members, often Native themselves, quietly protected the smallest rituals by braiding hair at night and smuggling stories into the classroom. And those who survived, those who returned home after years of separation, brought back fragments of knowledge, fragments of language, fragments of self.

Boarding schools represented a calculated attempt to rewrite Native identity from within. Families were torn apart; languages were criminalized; ceremony became a forbidden act. The Lower Sioux remained in place but were dispossessed internally, their children removed as surely as their land had been.

The damage was great and horrific. But it was not total.

After the Ashes

In Secret, the Sacred

Within the hardships held in Dakota memory, another story endured.

They remembered not only the war, but the hunger before it. The empty warehouses. The silence and treachery of the government agents. The words "Let them eat grass." The betrayal Indians felt was not sudden—it was the culmination of decades of broken faith. And in that memory, passed from elder to child, from winter lodge to summer fire, there remained not only sorrow—but resolve.

As federal laws criminalized ceremonies—like the Sun Dance, the potlatch, or the peyote ritual—many Tribal Nations adapted in secret. Sweat lodges were hidden in backwoods. Sacred bundles were buried beneath floorboards. Pipes were passed at night, under stars that looked on silently, as they always had.

Even as churches were built and children baptized, the drum never fully disappeared.

In some places, Christian prayers were spoken in Dakota or Ojibwe or Lakota, blending the old and new. In others, entire languages became vessels for survival—not just words, but memories encoded in grammar and metaphor.

The body of tradition was wounded, but the spirit of it flowed underground—like a river beneath snow, waiting.

Surviving the Middle Years

The 1880s and 1890s were years of maps without meaning. The land that had once moved with the People—following the migrations of buffalo herds, the seasons of planting and harvesting, the sacred movements of rivers and stars—was now chopped into rectangles. Reservations. Allotments. Sections and parcels with lines that made no sense to the earth. These boundaries were drawn not with respect, but with greed. They fenced in the spirit.

Under the Dawes Act of 1887, Tribal land was divided and allotted to individuals—160 acres for each "head of household," 80 for unmarried adults, 40 for orphans and children. What was left over—the so-called "surplus land"—was sold off to White settlers and developers. The law claimed to uplift Native People through private land ownership, to make them farmers and citizens in the mold of the American ideal.

But the Dawes Act was a blade hidden in the folds of a gift.

Most Indian people did not want their land divided. The Dawes Act ignored collective stewardship, communal grazing, and traditional use. It ignored kinship systems and seasonal practices. Many who received allotments were given land unfit for agriculture, or they lacked the resources to cultivate it. Others were swindled by unscrupulous agents or forced to lease their land at ruinous terms. Within decades, two-thirds of Native land had been lost.

A People once rich in territory, space, and sovereignty were made poor by paperwork.

And yet—they endured.

On the reservations, the days were hard and often joyless, but not meaningless. Families planted gardens and raised chickens.

They gathered roots and berries, hunted deer and fished riverbanks, often illegally, always carefully. They taught children what they could, in whispers. Some worked for local White ranchers or in government outposts, saving coins to buy horses or boots. Others found work in the Indian Service, attempting to navigate the system from within.

And slowly, a new generation began to rise—those who remembered the songs but also knew how to read the laws.

The Iron Thread of Memory

In Dakota camps and Ojibwe lodges, in Ho-Chunk homes and Ponca gatherings, the oral traditions survived. Elders passed down not only origin stories, but the recent histories—the names of treaty signers, the terms of the agreements, the betrayals that followed. Memory became a weapon against forgetting. And in these memories, seeds of justice were stored.

In many homes, a Bible sat next to a pipe. Children recited English lessons by day and heard star stories at night. Some converted to Christianity by choice. Others held fast to the old ways or found a balance between the two. There was no single path—but everywhere, resistance pulsed beneath the skin of the new reality.

Language was crucial. Though schools punished children for speaking it, the old words still found their way into lullabies and table conversation. A grandmother would say "wóiyaya" instead of "say that again." A grandfather would hum a song his own father had sung before the boarding school years. And in doing so, they kept the door cracked open.

By the early 1900s, many tribes had lost the legal claim to their land. But they had not lost their relationship to it.

The Drumbeat of Change

World War I marked an unexpected turning point. Native men volunteered in large numbers, many out of pride, some out of desperation. They served in France, in the trenches, in artillery units and as scouts. They fought for a country that had not fought for them. They bled beside White soldiers, even though they were not yet US citizens.

When they returned they carried more than war stories and medals on their chests. They brought back a sense of defiance. They had seen the world. They had seen nations respect them—as warriors, as equals. And they returned to find their own People still impoverished and disenfranchised.

The 1924 Indian Citizenship Act granted formal US citizenship to all Native Americans. On its face, it was a gift. In reality, it was a concession. Native People were now citizens, but they still lacked basic protections. In many states, they could not vote. They remained under the control of the Bureau of Indian Affairs. Their children still disappeared into boarding schools. Their lands remained at risk.

But some now learned how to organize.

Veterans began to speak at Tribal councils. Fledgling newspapers sprang up, printed in both English and Indian languages. Ceremonial societies reemerged under the guise of social clubs. Young men and women traveled to Washington, DC, to advocate for their People. The drum was no longer silenced—it was just muffled. And soon, it would rise again.

The Indian New Deal

In 1934, under pressure from reformers and Native leaders, Congress passed the Indian Reorganization Act (IRA). The law aimed to reverse the damage of the Dawes Act by restoring Tribal governments, halting land allotments, and encouraging cultural revitalization. Tribes were encouraged to draft constitutions, form business councils, and manage local affairs.

Not all tribes embraced the IRA. Some saw it as another form of control—forcing Indigenous governance into Western molds. But many saw opportunity.

Across Indian Country, Tribal councils emerged with new energy. Elections were held. Schools were reopened under Tribal leadership. Artists and weavers and ceremonial leaders began to share their work more freely. But there were still limits. There was still poverty. But the people were no longer entirely at the mercy of distant bureaucrats.

Many Indian Nations began, slowly, to again steer their own canoe.

The Seeds of Resistance

By mid-century, Indian Country was tired of being polite.

The promises of the Indian Reorganization Act had not lived up to their full potential. While some tribes gained better schools and elected councils, many remained trapped in poverty. The Bureau of Indian Affairs still controlled the purse strings. State governments encroached on Tribal rights. Health care, education, and housing on most reservations remained decades behind the rest of the country.

And then came Termination.

In 1953, the United States Congress passed House Concurrent Resolution 108—a policy known as "Termination." Its aim was to end the federal recognition of Tribal sovereignty altogether. Under the guise of "equality," Termination sought to dissolve Tribal governments, revoke federal trust responsibilities, and assimilate Native People fully into American society. In other words—erase them, legally.

Reservation lands were slated to be broken up, sold off, or handed to states. Health care services were to be discontinued. Tribes would no longer be sovereign Nations; they would simply be "Americans" living in rural poverty, without any land base or legal identity.

Over one hundred tribes and bands were targeted.

Some, like the Klamath of Oregon and the Menominee of Wisconsin, lost vast swaths of land, sacred forests and timber resources. The consequences were immediate and devastating. Unemployment soared, traditional Indian governments collapsed, and access to services vanished overnight.

But Termination also had an unintended effect.

It ignited a fire.

The Rise of Native Organizing

Native leaders—young and old, urban and reservation-based—began to organize like never before. National organizations like the National Congress of American Indians (NCAI) grew in influence, challenging federal policies and lobbying Congress directly. A new generation of Indigenous attorneys, scholars, and activists began to understand not just treaty rights, but the legal language of the colonizers.

Many had served in World War II or Korea. They had fought and bled for the United States, and they returned home to find their People still denied the rights they'd defended abroad. The contradiction was not just bitter—it was motivating.

Urban relocation programs had brought thousands of Native People into cities like Minneapolis, Chicago, Oakland, and Los Angeles. These programs, intended to break Tribal bonds, instead created urban Indian communities—dense networks of culture, resistance, and solidarity. In boarding houses, community centers, and late-night kitchen tables, a movement was born.

And in 1968, that movement found its drumbeat.

The American Indian Movement (AIM)

In a storefront on Franklin Avenue in Minneapolis—the same avenue that would one day appear in the buffalo hunter's dream—AIM was born.

The American Indian Movement, founded by Clyde Bellecourt, Dennis Banks, George Mitchell, and others, emerged as a voice of direct action. It was not a lobbying group. It was not a polite protest circle. It was warriors—urban warriors—demanding that the United States be held accountable for its promises and crimes.

AIM patrolled the streets to protect Native People from police violence. It occupied abandoned buildings and turned them into schools. It staged protests, sit-ins, and ceremonies in public spaces. They painted their faces red and raised their fists high. They were tired of invisibility. Tired of poverty. Tired of apologies.

And they were not alone.

Across Indian Country, other voices rose. The Red Power movement gathered force. The Trail of Broken Treaties in 1972 brought activists to Washington, DC, with a twenty-point manifesto. One year later, the Occupation of Wounded Knee—on the Pine Ridge Reservation in South Dakota—captured national headlines.

There, for seventy-one days, AIM and traditional Lakota elders held the US government at bay. They were surrounded by federal marshals and the FBI. Shots were fired. Lives were lost. But the story had changed.

No longer were Native People simply victims of history. They were now the authors of resistance.

Legal Victories, Spiritual Renewal

While the protests made headlines, other battles were fought in courtrooms.

Tribes began winning important legal cases. In Menominee v. United States (1968), the Supreme Court ruled that Tribal hunting and fishing rights had not been extinguished by Termination. In McClanahan v. Arizona State Tax Commission (1973), the court upheld Tribal sovereignty against state taxation.

Most crucially, in United States v. Washington (1974)—commonly known as the Boldt Decision—the court reaffirmed the right of tribes in the Pacific Northwest to fish in their "usual and accustomed places," securing 50 percent of the harvest. This landmark ruling restored not only economic power, but cultural lifeways.

Meanwhile, tribes reclaimed sacred ceremonies. In 1978, Congress passed the American Indian Religious Freedom Act, finally legalizing spiritual practices that had been suppressed for nearly a century.

Powwows, sweat lodges, vision quests, and Sun Dances—once outlawed—were now held again in the open. Songs were no longer whispered in shadows. They rang out beneath full moons and open skies.

The drumbeat was back.

Self-Determination Reclaimed

By the 1980s, a new framework had taken hold—Tribal self-determination. No longer would the federal government attempt to eradicate tribes. Instead, it would support their ability to govern themselves, manage their own resources, and shape their futures.

Under Presidents Nixon and Ford, and later under Carter and Reagan, new laws were passed that allowed tribes to run their own schools, administer housing programs, operate health clinics, and determine how federal funds would be spent.

It was not perfect. Sovereignty remained constrained, and many challenges remained. But something fundamental had shifted.

The Buffalo was not yet visible. But the hoofprints were forming. In many Tribal Nations, conversations began to stir—quiet ones, in council meetings and kitchen conversations.

What if economic independence was the next step in sovereignty?

What if the tools of business, when guided by tradition, could rebuild what was lost? What if a tribe could feed itself—not with rations or handouts—but with vision?

The Buffalo was coming back. Not as a beast of the prairie... but as something new.

The Emergence of the New Buffalo

Smoke Shops and Sovereignty

It started with tobacco. Not the sacred tobacco of the pipe, offered to the four directions. Not the tobacco grown in ceremony or given in prayer. This was commercial tobacco—sold in packs and cartons, sealed in plastic and stacked behind the counters of cinder block stores on reservation roads. Marlboros, Camels, and generics. Tax-free.

In the 1970s, as Tribal governments began to rediscover the power of self-determination, some of the first visible expressions came not from grand treaties or courtrooms, but from humble, often dusty smoke shops. These small stores, often housed in converted trailers or former church buildings, offered Native and non-Native customers discounted cigarettes and, in some cases, gas. They were open long hours, staffed by Tribal citizens, and operated on the fundamental principle that the reservation was sovereign land.

And sovereign land meant sovereign law.

States disagreed.

From Arizona to Minnesota, Oklahoma to Washington, Tribal smoke shops became contested ground. State tax agencies sent letters, filed suits, even dispatched agents to inspect records. They argued that tribes were selling tobacco to non-Native customers without collecting state excise taxes, thereby undercutting state-regulated businesses. The states wanted their share. The tribes wanted their rights.

It was not about cigarettes. Not really. It was about jurisdiction.

Was a reservation a part of the state—or was it a separate nation, as the treaties had once said?

The tribes remembered what the treaties had promised: the right to regulate their own commerce. The right to self-govern. The right to determine what happened on their lands.

And so, they stood their ground.

Standing Bear Smoke Shop

In upstate New York, on the Seneca Nation of Indians, the Standing Bear Smoke Shop became a lightning rod. Owned by a Seneca family, it offered cigarettes at a fraction of the cost of state-run outlets. State police began harassing drivers who purchased from the shop. Lawsuits followed. The Seneca Nation declared its authority to regulate trade on its territory—and banned state officials from entering Tribal land without permission.

In Oklahoma, the Cherokee Nation opened a Tribal tobacco enterprise and began producing its own brands, further asserting control. Other tribes followed: the Oneida, Ho-Chunk, and Shinnecock, among others.

Each smoke shop was a stand. A test. A statement.

And in many communities, they were also a lifeline.

Smoke shop revenues paid for emergency firewood deliveries, youth programs, and elder care. Some tribes used the money to reopen language classes or subsidize groceries. In places where federal funds were delayed or insufficient, tobacco money kept the lights on—literally and metaphorically.

But for Tribal governments, these shops weren't just revenue streams. They were assertions of memory. Reminders that despite centuries of removal, confinement, and betrayal, the People still had a say in what happened on their land.

Gas Wars and Border Tension

In Minnesota and Wisconsin, the "gas wars" began.

Tribes began selling untaxed gasoline to non-Native customers, often undercutting state fuel taxes by significant margins. Reservation gas stations posted prices ten, twenty, sometimes thirty cents cheaper per gallon than their off-reservation counterparts.

State officials fumed. Convenience store associations demanded crackdowns. Highway patrol units increased surveillance near reservation borders. Some Tribal gas station owners were arrested; others had their shipments blocked by state distributors acting under pressure.

But the tribes fought back—not with weapons, but with court filings and public campaigns.

In Lac du Flambeau, the Tribal council invoked its treaty rights and the sovereignty affirmed in the 1837 Treaty of St. Peters. In Red Lake, trucks rolled in under Tribal escort to deliver fuel directly to Tribally chartered businesses.

What once seemed like small roadside shops had now become flashpoints in a national legal and political battle over Native self-rule.

The Federal Response

The federal government, watching uneasily, often walked a tightrope.

On one hand, the U.S. Supreme Court had consistently affirmed that tribes possessed inherent sovereignty—especially in matters of internal commerce. On the other, Congress had allowed states increased jurisdiction through laws like Public Law 280, which transferred legal authority to certain state governments over tribes without consent.

The result was a landscape of contradictions.

In one state, a tribe could operate a gas station tax-free; in another, it could be sued. Some tribes negotiated compacts with states, agreeing to share revenues in exchange for legal peace. Others refused, seeing compromise as a slippery slope toward surrendering their hard-won autonomy.

Out of these tensions, a new concept began to take shape in Indian Country: the sovereignty economy.

This wasn't capitalism as the outside world knew it. It wasn't about shareholder dividends or private equity. It was about Tribal governments using enterprise to sustain the People. Every dollar made by a Tribal business—whether a smoke shop, a gas station, or a trading post—was reinvested into services, culture, and survival.

In this economy, sovereignty wasn't just legal theory. It was practice. It was everyday life. It was groceries delivered to an elder, a bus that took kids to school, a powwow pavilion rebuilt with local labor.

And it was growing.

Resource Management and Industry

Not all sovereignty was asserted at a storefront. Some came by river, by forest, by mountain. Some came through legal arguments about trees, fish, oil, and soil. Some came through quiet, patient reclamation—decades of knowing what was yours, even if no one else would say it aloud.

Where the federal government had tried to turn Tribal Nations into dependents, some tribes turned instead to their own land—the parts that hadn't been taken, the parts they could still fight for.

And from that land, they began to build.

The Timber People

In the mountains of eastern Arizona, the White Mountain Apache Tribe looked to its forests. Towering pines, old-growth timber, and deep ecological knowledge had shaped their culture for generations. But by the mid-20th century, much of their land had been mismanaged by the federal Bureau of Indian Affairs (BIA), which had awarded outside contracts with little Tribal input and questionable benefit.

The Apache leadership decided enough was enough.

They demanded control—not only over harvesting decisions, but over milling, reforestation, and profit allocation. In time, they created their own enterprise: White Mountain Apache Timber Company, one of the first full-scale, Tribally owned and operated timber industries in the country.

It wasn't just business. It was restoration.

Local employment soared. Apache foresters, trained in both traditional and modern methods, managed the health of the forest like a living relative. Revenues went toward schools, infrastructure, and housing. And in an era when "Indian management" was still mocked in Washington, the White Mountain Apache proved otherwise. They weren't just managing—they were thriving.

Their model spread. In Montana, the Confederated Salish and Kootenai Tribes followed suit, asserting control over their forestlands on the Flathead Reservation. Their logging operations, mill systems, and resource plans outperformed many state programs.

The message was clear: We are not passive. We are stewards. We know this land because we are of it.

Fish Wars and Sovereign Waters

In the Pacific Northwest, Tribal economies were rooted in the rivers. For the Yakama, Nisqually, Puyallup, and Lummi Nations, salmon fishing was not only sustenance—it was a sacred trust. Treaties signed in the 1850s had explicitly guaranteed "the right of taking fish, at all usual and accustomed places." But as decades passed, state governments ignored that promise. Fishing was restricted, Native fishermen were arrested, and their gear was confiscated.

The response wasn't immediate—but it was unforgettable.

In the 1960s and '70s, Native fishermen staged "fish-ins," inspired by the civil rights sit-ins of the South. They cast their nets and lines in forbidden places, daring the police to come. When they did, cameras rolled. Headlines followed.

Leaders like Billy Frank Jr., a Nisqually fisherman arrested more than fifty times, became symbols of defiance. His simple message—"We don't need a permit to fish on our own land"—cut through years of legal fog.

In 1974, the courts finally agreed. The Boldt Decision, as it became known, ruled that treaty tribes were entitled to up to 50 percent of the fish harvest and had co-management authority over fisheries.

This ruling sent shockwaves. It meant that Tribal Nations were not simply license holders. They were governments with equal status to the state—capable of setting regulations, managing ecosystems, and enforcing rules.

From the rivers came more than fish. Came identity. Came legal precedent. Came pride.

Minerals, Oil, and Legal Fences

In the Dakotas and the plains beyond, other tribes began asserting control over mineral rights. The Three Affiliated Tribes of the Fort Berthold Reservation in North Dakota—Mandan, Hidatsa, and Arikara—sat atop what would become the Bakken oil formation. For decades, outsiders had leased the land for pennies on the dollar, with no Tribal oversight and little environmental concern.

But in the 1970s, new leadership demanded change. They formed Tribal energy boards, hired engineers and attorneys, and began negotiating more aggressive terms. While the industry's long-term effects remain complex—and environmental costs are still debated—what changed was agency.

The tribes were no longer being extracted from. They were making the decisions.

Other tribes, such as the Southern Ute in Colorado, developed sophisticated natural gas operations and financial portfolios. By the 1990s, the Southern Ute were managing billion-dollar assets with a Tribal staff of trained economists, lawyers, and geologists.

They weren't just participating in capitalism. They were reshaping it on their terms.

Beyond the Earth – Early Industries and Innovation

Some Tribal Nations began industries entirely divorced from natural resources.

In South Dakota, the Oglala Lakota built a mobile home factory and a small electronics assembly plant. In Alaska, Native corporations—formed after the Alaska Native Claims Settlement Act of 1971—began investing in telecommunications, fisheries, and even software.

In North Carolina, the Eastern Band of Cherokee Indians created a business development authority and launched a chain of Tribally run convenience stores and hotels. Each one, though small, funneled money back into the community—and proved that tribes could build durable economies without depending on the federal government or outside investors.

Still, obstacles remained.

Bank loans were scarce. Many reservation lands could not be used as collateral because they were held in trust by the federal government. Infrastructure lagged. Roads were unpaved, power grids unreliable. And anti-Indian sentiment—especially in nearby rural counties—often sabotaged partnerships and scared off commercial interest.

But despite the odds, the foundations were being poured.

Smoke shops had declared the right to trade. Timber and fishing operations had reclaimed natural law. Energy developments had brought wealth… and new responsibilities.

Now, the talk in Tribal council chambers was changing. New questions were being asked:

What if we thought bigger?

What if we took control not just of land, but of law?

Not just of fish, but of finance?

What if we turned the sovereignty economy into a Buffalo?

The Road to Cabazon

The seeds of modern Tribal enterprise were scattered across many fields—timber, fisheries, tourism—but they began to sprout into something irreversible the moment the courts were forced to answer a fundamental question: How sovereign are Native Nations, really?

It wasn't a philosophical question anymore. It was financial. Legal. Urgent.

By the early 1980s, some tribes—still underfunded by the federal government and boxed out of surrounding economies—began experimenting with small-scale gaming operations. These were modest affairs: bingo halls, often run out of old gymnasiums or metal buildings. The jackpots weren't enormous, but they were bigger than what state law typically allowed, and that made them controversial.

The Cabazon Band of Mission Indians, a small tribe near Palm Springs, California, had lived through generations of marginalization.

Their reservation had no water lines, no sewer system, no paved roads. Federal aid was scarce, and state support was even scarcer. So the tribe decided to take matters into its own hands. They opened a card room and bingo parlor, using the profits to improve basic infrastructure and fund Tribal services.

The State of California responded with lawsuits.

Officials argued that the tribe was violating state gambling laws. The tribe countered that as a sovereign Nation they had the right to govern economic activity on their land—especially when that activity was legal under federal law and not explicitly prohibited by the state.

This dispute would climb through the courts, year by year, until it landed before the Supreme Court of the United States in 1986. The case was known as California v. Cabazon Band of Mission Indians, and it would change the course of Tribal sovereignty forever.

The Stakes of Sovereignty

The legal question boiled down to this: Could a state like California regulate gaming on Indian lands, even if the tribe didn't consent?

California argued yes. It claimed an interest in preventing crime, enforcing its public policies, and maintaining consistency across jurisdictions. But the Cabazon Band—and their attorneys—argued that this was not a simple issue of enforcement. It was about control. About dignity. About the right of a Nation to chart its own future, especially when no one else had provided the tools to survive.

Other tribes watched anxiously. So did Tribal legal scholars, sovereignty advocates, and federal officials who understood what was at stake. If the court sided with California, it would mark the beginning of a new era of state authority over Tribal lands. But if the court ruled for the Cabazon Band, it would affirm what many believed had always been true: Tribal Nations had the right to determine their own economic destiny.

In 1987, the court delivered its decision.

Cabazon won.

The justices ruled that California's laws regulating—but not outright prohibiting—gambling could not be applied to Tribal lands without the tribe's consent. More broadly, the court confirmed that Tribal sovereignty carried economic implications. If states could not impose their gambling laws, then tribes could operate gaming enterprises under their own authority—subject only to federal oversight.

The decision struck like lightning.

A door had opened. And hundreds of Tribal Nations would walk through it.

From BINGO to BILLIONS

The ruling in Cabazon was not just legal precedent—it was a signal. A signal that, for the first time in generations, tribes had a revenue mechanism that did not rely on federal appropriations, state handouts, or extractive industries.

Within months, other tribes began planning their own gaming operations. Some started with high-stakes bingo. Others explored poker rooms, small casinos, or gaming machines. The scale varied, but the intent was universal: to reclaim sovereignty through enterprise.

But as Tribal casinos emerged, so did tension.

State governments, seeing revenue flow away from their own lottery systems and regulated casinos, began pushing back. Some cited concerns about crime or addiction. Others, more bluntly, wanted a cut of the profits.

In response, Congress stepped in.

In 1988, lawmakers passed the Indian Gaming Regulatory Act (IGRA), a compromise measure intended to codify the parameters of Tribal gaming. It placed Tribal gaming into three categories:

- Class I: Traditional Tribal games with minimal prizes—regulated solely by the tribes.
- Class II: Bingo and certain card games—regulated by the tribes with federal oversight.
- Class III: Full-scale casino-style gaming—only allowed if the tribe negotiated a compact with the state.

IGRA was both a victory and a constraint.

On the one hand, it affirmed the right of tribes to operate gaming enterprises. On the other, it introduced a new legal maze: Tribal–state compacts that sometimes took years to negotiate, often under political and financial pressure. Some states acted in good faith. Others used the compact process to delay, restrict, or coerce tribes into revenue-sharing agreements that undermined their autonomy.

But despite the friction, the foundation had been laid.

A new Buffalo had been born.

The New Buffalo

Across the plains, the deserts, the forests, and coasts, the old buffalo had vanished long ago—its thunder silenced, its promise extinguished by greed, bullets, and railroads. For generations, its absence had been more than physical. It had been spiritual, economic, and cultural. With its disappearance came starvation, dislocation, and sorrow.

But now, something stirred.

In the smoke-filled halls of bingo parlors, in the flickering lights of slot machines, in the steady hum of new construction rising on Tribal lands, a new spirit took form. One not of hide and horn, but of law, negotiation, and resilience. It was called the New Buffalo—and it moved not across prairie grass, but through bank ledgers and Tribal compacts.

It came in response to a single question: What does sovereignty look like when you're no longer starving?

For decades, Indigenous people had been told that self-determination was a noble dream, but an impractical one. That dependency was inevitable. That poverty was a condition of their identity. Gaming shattered that lie.

Within a decade of the Cabazon decision and the passage of IGRA, Tribal gaming became the fastest-growing segment of the gaming industry in the United States. Small-scale bingo halls gave way to full-fledged casino resorts, many of which rivaled those in Las Vegas and Atlantic City.

By the early 2000s, Tribal gaming had grown into a multi-billion-dollar industry.

And it wasn't just about money.

A New Era of Tribal Self-Governance

Revenue from gaming enterprises flowed directly to Tribal governments, many of which had never had significant discretionary budgets before. For the first time in living memory, Tribal councils could fund their own schools, build their own clinics, pave their own roads.

Language programs once on the verge of extinction found new lifelines. Cultural preservation projects were launched. Housing for elders was built. Youth programs expanded. In some communities, dropout rates fell. In others, life expectancy began to rise.

Some tribes used revenue to buy back ancestral lands—reversing, acre by acre, the theft of centuries. Others invested in renewable energy, tourism, or financial portfolios to reduce long-term dependence on gaming.

And critically, gaming revenue allowed tribes to hire and retain Native professionals—lawyers, doctors, engineers, educators—creating internal economies that had been impossible just a generation before.

Rebuilding the Circle

The symbolism was powerful. In the old ways, the buffalo had been everything: shelter, food, clothing, story. When it was taken, so too was the circle of life it supported. Gaming, while a modern tool, helped to mend that circle—not in the same form, but with the same intent—to provide.

Still, the road was not easy.

Gaming brought power, but also pressure. Tribes faced external scrutiny, internal debate, and frequent legal challenges. Non-Native communities sometimes resented Tribal success, particularly when new casinos drew tourism and revenue away from nearby towns.

In some cases, state governments attempted to tax or regulate Tribal gaming, despite its sovereign protection. These efforts often led to new lawsuits, many of which again affirmed Tribal rights, but not without cost, conflict, and delay.

Even within tribes, disagreements emerged. Some elders worried that casinos were spiritual distractions. Others feared cultural dilution, or overdependence on an industry tied to human weakness. These were real concerns. And in many places, they were addressed with care.

Tribes built casinos that reflected their values—featuring Native art, locally sourced materials, and cultural programming. Many required that employees take part in cultural training or language immersion. Some reserved a portion of profits for sacred site preservation, repatriation efforts, or traditional governance systems.

Tribal gaming, when wielded with vision, became more than business. It became a spiritual restoration.

Winners and Critics

By 2020, there were more than 500 Tribal gaming operations in the United States, owned by over 240 federally recognized tribes. Total revenue surpassed $30 billion annually, supporting over 700,000 jobs—many of them for Native employees.

And yet, critics remained.

Some argued that gaming created inequality between tribes—those with advantageous locations near cities or highways flourished, while remote tribes struggled to compete. Others worried about problem gambling, corruption, or the perception that Native identity was being defined through commerce.

But most Tribal leaders responded with clarity.

Gaming is not identity, they said. It is a tool. A bridge. A means to an end.

And the end was not greed. It was sovereignty.

Sovereignty that meant clean water, safe housing, functioning schools, and cultural resurgence. Sovereignty that meant hiring your own attorneys instead of depending on Bureau of Indian Affairs lawyers. Sovereignty that meant dignity in negotiation—whether with states, the federal government, or international visitors.

The Buffalo Was Back

It did not bellow or stampede. It moved in data, strategy, and quiet transformation. But in its own way, it returned. And in its shadow, Native Nations stood taller.

PART 2:
LEONARD

The Boy Who Climbed the Cottonwood

Long before Leonard Prescott would speak before councils, guide his People through legal labyrinths, and stand at the forefront of a movement that would alter the future of Tribal Nations, he was just a five-year-old boy with five siblings in Morton, Minnesota, growing up in the Mdewakanton band of the Dakota tribe. He had more spirit than sense and a sky-high cottonwood tree outside his front door.

The name Mdewakanton (Mid-uh-WAH-kan-ton) came from the Dakota name "Mdawaken," meaning "Lake of the Ancient Spirits" or "Spirit Lake." In other words, "those who dwell at the spirit lake."

Morton was not much to look at in those days. The house that Leonard's family lived in was barely more than a frame—two rooms, no running water, a stove that groaned through the brutal winters with temps dropping to -40° F, and a path to the outhouse that seemed endless in the snow. Yet, inside that humble home, the Prescott family endured.

Leonard was the oldest of three boys, just younger than his three sisters. Together they shared a bed while their parents, Herbert and Rose Blossom Prescott, slept on a cot in the living room. Herbert laid bricks to feed the family of eight. Rose Blossom melted snow to make water. It was a life built on determination, not complaint.

Behind the house stretched a forest that to Leonard's young eyes might as well have been endless. The family fetched water from a spring a half mile away, passing a tiny schoolhouse where his sisters studied—two rooms, whitewashed, quiet. But the most imposing presence in Leonard's world stood not out back, but out front—a towering cottonwood tree that rose just fifteen feet from their door.

To Leonard, the tree was not simply tall—it was magnificent. Its bark, gnarled and thick, seemed like the skin of an ancient beast. Its branches thrashed in the wind like the arms of a giant. It was, to a boy born under open skies and dreaming of wide worlds, a challenge. An invitation.

One day, when his parents left to run errands, they passed to him the casual admonition that carried more weight than any five-year-old should bear. "Leonard, you're the man of the house now."

This time, he believed them.

He waited until the wind calmed. The sun cast long shadows across the yard. The cottonwood loomed silently. Then, with a courage born of both innocence and defiance, Leonard reached for the bark and began to climb.

First one branch, then another. He hoisted himself higher than he'd ever dared, grunting with effort, skin scraping against bark. Each branch was thinner than the last, each step more dangerous. But he climbed on—past the roofline, past his own fear—until the branches swayed in the wind and the sky unfolded around him like a page from a book he could not yet read.

For a moment, he did not think of his bed shared with five siblings, or the walk to the outhouse, or the frozen silence of winter mornings. He thought only of the view. And what he saw was not just rooftops and railroad tracks—it was something beyond. It was possibility. Space. A land that belonged to him and his People, even if no one else would admit it.

Maybe it was a glimpse of the future. Maybe it was the spirit of the cottonwood whispering. Maybe it was the earliest flicker of a vision inspired by family tales of vast buffalo herds, now absent from the landscape, that would one day become the foundation of a modern Buffalo to replace the old.

But dreams have gravity, and trees are no place to stay.

A gust of wind snapped him back to the moment. The tree rocked. Leonard froze, hands clamped around a slender branch that no longer felt so sturdy. The climb up had been glorious. The climb down looked impossible.

He called out for help.

His sisters—Mary, Patricia, Rayann—panicked. They ran to the Lucio family's home, a quarter mile down the road. The call went to the Redwood Falls Fire Department. Time dragged on, the cottonwood swaying beneath the boy's desperate grip. By the time the fire truck arrived, Leonard's arms were shaking, and his heart thudded like a drum.

A fireman raised the ladder slowly, carefully, and met the boy's wide eyes with calm. "Trust me," he said, and Leonard, trembling, let go.

Down on the ground, he was safe—but transformed. His mother scolded him. His father laughed, gently. But Leonard had done something few dared at five years old: he had faced fear, climbed beyond it, and glimpsed something more. He had shown his siblings—perhaps even himself—that going where others will not is the first act of leadership.

That cottonwood would remain in his memory not just as a tree, but as a turning point. The first summit. A teacher with no voice but a powerful lesson—the higher you climb, the more clearly you can see what must be changed—and how far you have to go to change it.

Leonard Prescott would go far. But even in the council chambers, even in the negotiations that brought life to Mystic Lake and beyond, a part of him still stood in the branches of that tree—eyes filled with wind and wonder, seeing what others could not yet imagine.

Family Life On the Reservation

The Inheritance of Names and Wound

Leonard Prescott was not merely given a name—he inherited it. As the eldest son, he carried his father's full name—Herbert Leonard Prescott, a man carved by war, tradition and silence. Herbert had been raised on the Lower Sioux Reservation in Minnesota, the son of David and Mary Prescott, both full-blooded Dakota. David had once been a leader—Tribal chairman in the 1950s—and his brother, Albert, followed a similar path, guiding the community through the uncertainty of the 1960s. In Leonard's bloodline, leadership ran deep. But it also ran scarred.

Herbert Prescott had served his country aboard a navy ship in World War II, but he would never speak of it—not of the experience, of the wound, or of the three-inch scar etched along his face like a memory he refused to name. He never said how he got that scar, and Leonard learned not to ask.

There were signs, though—glimpses into the broken places inside the man. Herbert admired Ira Hayes, the Pima Nation US Marine who helped raise the flag on Iwo Jima and later died of alcoholism. Leonard would later realize why. Hayes, too, had returned home from war to a country that honored his service in public but abandoned his humanity in private. Herbert saw himself in that mirror.

When he did work, Herbert poured concrete—sidewalks for schools in Morton, projects on the reservation. But work was inconsistent. Life after war was harder than life before. The Prescott family lived modestly, and the heaviness of postwar America settled differently on Native families—silently, pervasively.

Then came the car crash.

Herbert was driving. The children were with him. It was an ordinary day until it wasn't. Mary, Leonard's sister, suffered severe injuries to her mouth and lost several teeth. She became withdrawn after that. She pulled inward, away from crowds and comfort. Leonard believed, in hindsight, that this early trauma shaped her later struggles. Alcohol, for her, became a disguise—an elixir to make the pain tolerable and to reveal, if only for a few hours, the girl who might have been.

Pat, another sister, suffered grave injuries to her legs. She was hospitalized for weeks in Redwood Falls. Herbert, already drinking, began drinking even more heavily. The accident added another layer to his unspoken pain. He stopped seeking permanent work. He brooded. He remembered war. And he drank.

Yet through it all, Herbert Prescott remained proud of his service—deeply proud—but also embittered by how his country repaid him with distance, suspicion and silence. His wife, Rose, understood his despondency better than most. She had grown up on the Upper Sioux Reservation just as he had grown up on the Lower. They had met as teenagers, at powwows and community gatherings, where the old dances still echoed and new love sometimes sparked.

Rose was five-eighths Dakota, descended from Lilly and Alex, and not directly tied to the bands involved in the 1862 uprising. Over time, these fractions of Dakota blood among community members would become a major issue. Rose brought warmth and resolve into the family—an anchor amid turbulence. The Prescott household was small, crowded, and alive with laughter and tension, like most households on the reservation in those days.

Their home stood near a gully, and to a child's eyes it was a wilderness of wonder. Gophers tunneled beneath the yard like spirits. Leonard once watched his dog, a white-water Springer Spaniel named Butch, lunge after a gopher that had bitten him on the lip. The dog thrashed wildly until the gopher fell still, a tiny drama in the natural order—a boy's first lesson in predator and prey.

That wasn't the only memory etched into the landscape. There was also the church. At four years old, Leonard went with his family to Samuel Pond Church nestled within the reservation. It was there, of all places, that he first experienced fear. Not of God nor the preacher, but of Santa Claus.

The red-suited figure was meant to be magical, but to Leonard, the looming figure was terrifying. When the time came to sit on Santa's lap, Leonard fled—down the center aisle, out into the snow-covered lot, and straight into the car. His parents, thinking him just cold and shy, came out to start the engine and warm him while the program continued. But Leonard, curled against the door and fast asleep, was jolted awake when the door opened and he tumbled out, striking his head on a rock. He woke up later with stitches and a colorful story.

Lessons from the Land and the Red Road

The reservation at that time was not large, but for Leonard it held an entire world.

Out front, beyond the cottonwood tree and the narrow gravel road, there lay a deep gully. It was wild in the way small places can be wild to children. Frogs gathered there by the hundreds in the spring—green ones, brown ones, with throats that pulsed like drums in the dusk. Leonard, no more than a boy, would crouch in the weeds, trying to catch them with his bare hands. One day, he spotted a frog sitting still, barely breathing. He crept forward quietly, fingers ready to pounce.

But he wasn't the only one hunting.

A snake had also fixed its gaze on the frog. Leonard turned his head just in time to see the serpent strike. It moved with brutal elegance—silent, certain, unstoppable. One moment the frog was there. The next, it was gone.

Leonard said nothing. He just watched.

The memory stayed with him long after the gully dried up and the frogs grew scarce. It became, in time, one of his first metaphors for life—not one learned from books or teachers, but from the land itself. That day, he understood something elemental—*the strong do not always win, but they usually do*. And unless the small and the vulnerable learn to be clever, quick, or united, they will be consumed.

That truth had echoed through generations of Dakota history. It was etched in the broken treaties, in the community's ever-shrinking land base, in the quiet funerals of languages no longer spoken. It was a lesson Little Crow himself had learned too late. In the years before the US–Dakota War of 1862, Little Crow—then a chief trying to lead his People through impossible choices—realized that diplomacy and decency were no match for betrayal and steel.

Leonard, still young, could feel the distant thunder of that past war in the silence of the elders—not spoken, but always there. It was present in every road sign that bore a White name. In every strip of land fenced off and deeded to someone else. The treaties that had promised permanence had become pause buttons, nothing more—agreements written only to last until the next wave of settlers arrived.

And they kept arriving.

The land was taken from them. Their culture too. Piece by piece. Through force, yes, but also through seduction—the promise of something better. A better way to live, a better God, a better name, a better tongue. The promises were always of something better, but never *theirs*.

The "red road"—the spiritual path of the People—was not a concept that Leonard as a child had fully understood. But as he grew, he began to glimpse its meaning. The red road was not paved or painted. It was *lived.* And it was marked by the redness of blood—the blood of ancestors, the blood of sacrifice, the blood of choices made under pressure.

Tradition held that as one walks this red road through life, one passes between two forces. On one side… destruction, selfishness, despair. On the other… generosity, protection, gratitude to the Creator. And every step is a decision.

Leonard saw how easy it was to stray. His own People, at times, wandered off that road—seduced by alcohol, numbed by hopelessness, led astray by the false lights of someone else's dream. The path of assimilation into the White man's culture offered comfort at first glance. But deeper in, it was a maze, and many never found their way back.

And yet, Leonard never judged them. How could he? He had seen the traps laid for his People. He had seen how sadness and anger were handed down like heirlooms—how they crept into the blood and sat at the family table.

This sorrow wasn't just personal. It was national.

It had crept into the hearts of children too—children who learned English but forgot their grandmothers' prayers. Children who were taught to be grateful for schools that denied their identity. Children who were told that their land was taken for their own good. Leonard saw it clearly. This was not just conquest. It was a systematic *unmaking*.

And yet, the root still lived.

Earth and Sky, Root and Tree

In Dakota teachings, the world is not made of strangers. It is made of relatives. The animals, the rivers, the wind—all are kin. And in that understanding is a truth so vast it cannot be contained in a classroom or treaty. It is a truth lived. Mother Earth, they say, is not a metaphor. She is the literal provider—of food, of water, of medicine, of balance. Her body is the land. Her blood is the rivers. Her breath, the wind. She feeds us even now, though we have wounded her in so many places.

As a boy, Leonard was taught that the old way—the truly old way—meant depending on the land with reverence. It meant knowing how to hear what the trees said before they fell. It meant taking only what you needed. It meant gathering not only berries or firewood, but stories. Wisdom. Songs. The world was alive, and that meant everything mattered.

Father Sky also was not simply a direction. He was the home of the sun, the keeper of light, the source of the stars. And between them—earth below, sky above—walked human beings, blessed with the rarest gift of all—a mind. The mind to create. To remember. To choose.

That gift came with danger. A human mind could choose to make war. It could choose to forget. It could build cities where rivers once sang and leave nothing but concrete scars. But it could also do something else—it could build Nations. It could restore what had been broken. It could remember its place.

The traditional way of life, Leonard knew, was no longer fully available to his People. The buffalo no longer darkened the plains.

The songs were fewer now. The language, once spoken in every home, now had to be taught with worksheets and recordings. The world had changed, but not all was lost.

What remained was the will. The capacity to adapt without surrender. The power to write new law grounded in old memory. To write policy not to mimic the outside world, but to preserve what mattered. To govern as Native People—not merely as administrators, but as caretakers.

In time, Leonard would come to understand that sovereignty is not something granted. It is something exercised. He would help build institutions, draft laws, defend principles that others called outdated but which he knew were eternal. He understood that Tribal government was not about hierarchy. It was about survival, responsibility, and kinship.

It was about the root.

He thought often of the trees on the reservation. Some grew tall and strong. Others bent in the wind. But no tree stood without a root. And in his community, Leonard came to see that he was not the tallest. He was not the most visible. But he could be the root—hidden, steady, grounding the future in something unshakable.

Leadership, he knew, was not about glory. It was about endurance. About holding fast to memory when others let go. About ensuring that the path his People walked—whether called sovereignty, survival, or the red road—would still be there for those yet unborn.

The cottonwood tree still stood near where the house once was. The gully had changed. The frogs were fewer. The world had moved on. But beneath the soil, the root still lived. And because of that, so did the People.

The Melting Pot

Leaving Morton

By the time Leonard Prescott was six, the land that had shaped him was already beginning to recede behind him. Morton, with its cottonwood tree, its gopher-hunting dogs, and its quiet Dakota rituals carried out in the shadows of postwar hardship, would always be the place of origin. But it would not be the place of becoming.

In pursuit of something *more*—more work, more services, more security—his parents packed up their six children and left the reservation behind. What they sought in Saint Paul, the capital city of Minnesota, was the promise whispered to many Indian families in the 1950s and '60s—opportunity. The streets might not be paved with gold, but they held the possibility of plumbing, wages, schools, and the kind of upward mobility that reservation life—shaped by historical violence and government neglect—rarely afforded.

They arrived in the Selby-Dale neighborhood, a patchwork of working-class homes and apartment blocks woven with tension and motion. The Prescotts moved into the bottom floor of a duplex on Carroll Avenue, and the world changed overnight. Morton had been rural and insulated. This place was teeming. Black families,

Mexican-American families, a few White renters, and scattered Native relatives from other bands all shared these few square blocks. The rules were unwritten but clear. Boundaries existed—not just of race, but of street, of pride, of pain.

Leonard could feel the shift most in his father.

In Morton, Herbert Prescott had once been the unspoken head of the household—even if wounded, even if troubled. But in Saint Paul, the weight of breadwinning shifted. Rose Blossom, Leonard's mother, took a job as a nurse's aide at Anchor Hospital—the same hospital where she had once stood vigil beside her daughter Pat after the car accident. Now, she worked nights to support the family, returning exhausted to care for children who needed her just as much at home as the family needed her paycheck.

Herbert, meanwhile, became less of who he had been. Or at least he seemed to feel it. Work was sparse. Pride eroded. He turned more often to alcohol, and the children began to see him not as a stable figure but as a ghost of something more powerful that used to be. The household began to orbit Rose, even as Herbert drifted into himself.

But Leonard was still watching.

Becoming a Street Child

The Selby-Dale neighborhood had no elders guiding from firelight. It had curbs and corners, trash bins and pawn shops. It had women standing on street corners long after dark, laughter that rose from behind closed doors, and music that bled into the night from unseen rooms. This was not Morton. It was something else—raw, unpredictable, alive.

Leonard took it in like a second breath. He began to understand the code of the city not through formal lessons, but through bruises and running feet. The kids in the neighborhood were quick with fists and quicker with judgment. Fights were not rare—they were regular, even expected. The groups were formed by race and territory, sometimes by bloodline, sometimes by sheer instinct. Blacks, Mexicans, Whites, and even other Indians fought for footing, identity, and respect. It didn't matter if you understood why you were fighting. You fought, or you were marked.

Leonard and his family moved often to other quarters, sometimes just blocks at a time. He never knew exactly why—whether it was rental disputes, eviction notices, or just lower rent somewhere else. With each move came a reshuffling of loyalties and threats. But beneath it all, his father's longing for Morton never faded. On occasion, they would return to the reservation, Herbert aching to reclaim something he could never quite hold again.

There were moments when Leonard still tried to understand manhood in the shape of his father. Herbert, despite his wounds, still clung to symbols of strength. He worshipped Joe Louis, the great Black heavyweight champion. On Friday nights, when televised boxing aired, Herbert would drag Leonard into the armchair beside him, refusing to let him leave for street games or neighborhood mischief.

"You don't want to be a man?" he'd ask gruffly. During the fights, his emotions—amplified by drink—would rise and spill. He'd punch Leonard's arm with his knuckles, harder than necessary, then mock his son's tears.

Leonard never knew if it was intended as discipline or just something more confused—some desperate attempt by his father to graft toughness onto his son. But even as his arm ached, Leonard filed away the lesson of pain.

There were other lessons too. School, while not hostile, was alien. Kindergarten and first grade came and went without note, but by second grade, Leonard had begun forming bonds with Mexican kids, Black kids, even some White ones. Still, he knew the boundaries. There were lines you didn't cross. These were not written or spoken, but enforced nevertheless.

The streets taught him how to walk a certain way. The city taught him to keep his eyes open. And his own guilt, sharpened through one unforgettable act, taught him about shame.

It began with a desire he hadn't known how to name—a longing to be like the other kids. They had candy. Toys. Sodas from the corner store. Leonard had none of that. And so, one night, as his mother left her purse open on the couch, he reached inside and pulled out a bill thinking it was a dollar.

It wasn't.

Upstairs, under the yellow light of a bedroom lamp, he unfolded it. Ten dollars! A fortune. He felt sick.

He thought about giving it back. He thought about spending it. But he did neither. And as time went by, the window had closed, and his mother had begun to notice. Bills went unpaid. Accusations followed. First, the landlord, then the electrician. Eventually, all six children were summoned to the attic for interrogation.

"This is going to hurt me more than you," Rose said, and began the rounds with a belt.

Leonard said nothing.

Rayann, unable to bear the silence, eventually pointed to Alan. "He always steals," she said. Alan denied it. The punishment paused. Leonard remained quiet. And for reasons he never fully understood—favoritism, fatigue, or divine mercy—he was spared that night.

But not from himself.

A month passed. The ten-dollar bill burned in his pocket like a secret shame. Then one day, he brought it to his second-grade teacher, Mrs. Anderson, a tall woman with soft eyes and golden hair who had always shown him kindness. "I want to pay for my books," he said.

She raised an eyebrow. "This is too much," she said.

"I want to pay for everyone's books," Leonard added, trying to sound noble, to fix what he'd done.

Mrs. Anderson looked at him a long moment. "Did your mother give this to you?"

He paused, then said no.

She called his parents.

The walk home was long. He dragged a stick along a chain-link fence, trying to stretch the minutes before he'd have to open the door and face the two people whose trust he'd broken. When he did, they were waiting—silent, fixed, immovable.

He was punished. Grounded. Sent to bed without food. He lay there, night after night, smelling supper from the next room, listening to laughter from which he was excluded. And though the punishment stung, what hurt most was knowing Mrs. Anderson had snitched. He had trusted her. But he also knew she had been right.

It took a couple of years to drum up the courage to try again—pilfering from his father. He was bent on obtaining some money for the kinds of things his friends enjoyed. He'd heard coins jingling in the pockets of his father's pants. Nine-year-old Leonard reached for them, but Herbert was awake. Leonard didn't make it far—and paid the price.

These moments, small in the scale of a life, were monumental in shaping Leonard's conscience. They didn't just teach him that stealing was wrong. They taught him something deeper—that the world was built on trust, and that when trust breaks, something sacred cracks with it.

He learned, too, that poverty wasn't just hunger or hand-me-down shoes. It was wanting something so badly you were willing to hurt the people who loved you. And that guilt, once planted, grows roots.

But these experiences—these private failures—did something else as well. They taught Leonard to notice the suffering of others. They gave him a sensitivity that would later evolve into advocacy. It was from these early cracks that his sense of justice, of collective responsibility, would begin to form.

He would never forget how it felt to be small in a city of noise. But he would also never forget how to listen for the quiet… and how to carry what others had dropped.

Stark Realities

Chaos at Home

Around this time, back in the small, shifting homes of Saint Paul, weekends became rituals of contradiction. They started with music and ended in bruises. Friends and relatives would come over. There'd be beer and whiskey, laughter and card games. The sound of country music drifted from the radio or the record player. The kitchen would fill with the voices of women preparing food and trading stories, while the men argued over hands and bets.

Then, slowly, the mood would shift.

"You cheated!" someone would yell.

"I didn't cheat—you did!"

The card table would upend. Paper bills would scatter across the floor like dry leaves. The women, already weary, would mutter, "Take it outside." And so the men would spill into the small yard, fists clenched, voices raised, egos colliding under the flickering porch light.

Inside, the children watched—not with fear, but with a sort of resigned expectation. It had happened before. It would happen again. They didn't cry. They didn't hide.

While waiting for the storm to pass, the children would scramble to the floor and scoop up as much loose money as they could. For a few moments, the macho chaos was profitable.

But the worst of it came when the fights followed Dad back into the house. He'd accuse Mom of flirting, or worse—of shaming him in front of others. She'd defend herself, steady but firm. He'd shout louder. She'd push back. Then he'd hit her.

When that happened, Rose Blossom changed. She'd roll her head side to side, moaning, as if caught between worlds. Her body remained upright, but her mind slipped into some unreachable place. She seemed to fall into a trance—unreachable even to her children. No words could reach her. No touch could pull her back.

Eventually, Dad would leave the room, sometimes the house. The kids would gather around their mother, whispering, coaxing, praying. After a time, her breathing would slow. Her eyes would clear. And she would ask, in the same soft voice as always, "Can I have a cigarette? Some coffee?"

That was when they knew she had returned.

Violence, Heroes, and Moral Reckonings

It was under the skeleton of a half-built highway in 1962 that Leonard Prescott first began to confront the unpredictable violence of city life. He was around eleven years old. His brother, Robbie, was a couple years younger. The two of them had been walking under a bridge where US Highway 94 was being carved into the landscape—an exposed artery of urban ambition—when a group of Black kids cornered them.

"What are you doing walking in our territory?" one of them asked, grabbing Leonard by the arms. Two boys held him while another picked up a 2x4, a jagged piece of wood left behind by construction workers. Robbie, without thinking, peeled off his shoe and leapt to Leonard's defense. The older boys caught his hand and yanked the shoe away.

"This shoe's too hard to hit him with," one of them joked, tossing it aside.

But before anything worse could happen, salvation arrived. Linda Jefferson, a girl a few years older, half Ojibwe and half Black, appeared like a spirit sent from the sky. Her voice cut through the tension. "What are you guys doing? I know these two boys. Leave them alone."

The older kids recognized her name—Linda Jefferson's family was respected in the neighborhood. Without another word, they dropped the board and faded back into the shadows. Linda walked Leonard and Robbie to safety, guiding them toward the Overboy's Club, where they'd been heading all along.

That day lingered in Leonard's heart. Not just for the fear, or the rage he swallowed, but for the way Linda had stepped in—strong, certain, protective. That night, and many nights after, Leonard imagined being like her. Or better still—being like Superman. He religiously watched the new TV series about that extraterrestrial with superpowers. The cape. The strength. The speed. The ability to fly. To save the world. He didn't just admire that superhero. He needed to become one.

But the world had more lessons in store.

Later that year, Leonard's mother gave him the responsibility of taking his little brother, Alan, to the movies. Rayann, the older sister, tagged along. Each child was given a quarter—a good good amount of money in those days… enough to see three features at the Lyceum Theatre. But across the street, the Strand was playing something Leonard had longed to see—*Pinocchio*. The ticket cost seventy-five cents—more than he had, but not more than the combined quarters in his pocket.

He wept. Pleaded. And eventually, out of love or guilt or both, Rayann and Alan gave him their quarters.

"You go," they said. "We'll wait outside."

Inside the Strand, Leonard found a seat in the balcony and stared up at the screen. But within ten minutes, the magic vanished. The puppets still danced and the projected image still flickered, but he couldn't concentrate. The weight of selfishness pressed on him like a hand to the chest. He slipped out early, found Rayann and Alan still waiting, and walked home silently.

Later, the memory soured further. He came to understand that what his siblings had offered wasn't just pocket change. It was reverence. Trust. A kind of faith in him as the eldest, the one they looked to. In betraying that, Leonard felt something crack inside. He had taken their kindness and fed it to his hunger. The lesson sank deeply into him—*it is worse to take from the generous than from the stingy.*

Meanwhile, at home, things were unraveling.

Phoenix Heat and West Side Lessons

In the summer of 1960, Leonard's path veered south. His family decided to move to Phoenix, Arizona, seeking a fresh start. They arrived into a wave of desert heat that felt like a furnace. The temperature was 110 degrees, a suffocating wall of air that hit harder than anything Leonard had ever felt in Minnesota.

The family settled into a place of their own. Leonard's mother enrolled him into sixth grade at Ann Ott Elementary, where the air conditioning didn't always work, and most of the students were brown—but not Indian. They were Mexican-American, and their world had its own customs, rhythms, and dangers.

Leonard was used to street conflict, but in Phoenix, the rules were different. He stuck out, and not in a good way. His light-brown skin and straight, black hair marked him as *other*, but not clearly enough to belong. He made a few friends, mostly quiet boys who didn't ask questions, but he never settled in. The city didn't feel like home. The dry heat, the vast boulevards, the unfamiliar voices—it all felt far away from the wet trees of Minnesota, the pulse of Selby Avenue and the chaos of the Snake Pit. By March, they headed home.

Frequent Moves

Over the years, they didn't just move to different houses. It seemed they moved to new galaxies. Leonard can recall at least a dozen streets throughout Saint Paul, including Carroll Avenue, Inglehart, Marshall, Hauge Avenue, Pleasant, Robert Street, Atwater, Concord, University, and Snelling. The moves blended into one another. There was no stable center, only fragments of places where love, pain, and confusion were unpacked and repacked again.

By the time Leonard turned thirteen, the family moved again—this time to the lower west side where his Uncle Gilbert had relocated after leaving the reservation. The west side was largely Mexican-American, anchored in a history of laborers and railroad families. The area was being transformed into an industrial zone called "the flats." But for Leonard, it was just another neighborhood with new faces, new rules, but the same ghosts.

After years of turmoil, Rose Blossom asked for a divorce. Herbert moved back to Morton. Sometimes he would hop freight trains to Seattle, Phoenix, or other cities he had drifted through before—places where skid rows stretched for blocks and the air smelled like last chances.

Paper Routes and the Snake Pit

Leonard Prescott's first taste of earning his own money came at the age of twelve. His friends, Richard and Geno Flores, had been selling newspapers downtown in Saint Paul and encouraged

Leonard and his brother Al to join them. It was a chance not only to earn but to carve out a piece of independence in a world that offered little.

In the beginning, Leonard was assigned to the least desirable corners—quiet stretches of 4th and Minnesota Street, or the lonely edge of 5th and Robert. There weren't many customers there, just echoes off the cold brick and the sound of passing buses. But the paperboys worked on seniority. In time, Leonard would earn his way to the more coveted spots: corners in front of bars, where coins flowed more freely and tips were part of the transaction.

One of the prime locations was the Exchange Bar, known on the street—and by Leonard's own relatives—as "The Snake Pit." It was a bar thick with stories, most of them rough, some ridiculous, but all unforgettable. Leonard would walk in with his stack of papers, call out, "Paper, ma'am? Paper, sir?" and work his way through the narrow aisle between tables.

The people were varied—blue-collar laborers, White men in neckties, regulars half-slumped from drink, and one old White woman, long drunk and toothless, who always called Leonard over to hug and kiss him. He hated it. But she always tipped well.

The bar's reputation had been earned. One night, a man named Lefty Bongo, a familiar character among the regulars, suddenly leapt onto the bar, screaming about imaginary grasshoppers crawling over his body. He ran its entire length, swatting at the invisible swarm before police arrived and carted him out in a straitjacket. For Leonard, the bar was like watching a live-action movie—chaotic, unpredictable, and strangely thrilling.

When Leonard and Al first started, newspapers sold for seven cents, and the boys made a two-cent profit per paper. When the price rose to ten cents, their cut was supposed to go up to three cents—but something changed. Customers, accustomed to handing over a dime for a seven-cent paper, had been effectively tipping them an extra three cents. Now that the paper cost ten cents, they continued giving a dime—but with no surplus.

The profit margin disappeared.

Still, Leonard learned how to make the system work. Louie Manouch, the paper master, and his assistant, Reggie, kept things in motion. If you were smart, you claimed the bar corners. Patrons leaving with drinks in their bellies were more likely to toss a paperboy a quarter. But territory was always under threat. Other boys tried to muscle in. Sometimes it ended in fights, the kind that taught fast lessons about territory, toughness, and silence.

Leonard worked Saturday nights, selling early Sunday editions until ten or eleven o'clock—sometimes later. At home, money was scarce. There wasn't always food on the table, not even bread or potatoes. So when Leonard came home, he gave his earnings to his parents. That, more than the work itself, made him feel proud.

Some bar patrons, startled by the sight of a child out so late, would ask, "If we buy all your papers, will you go home now?" Leonard always said yes. And when they did buy out his stack, he would leave the bar… and find another one. The city had many, and Leonard had a route to run.

He learned patience there. Patience with drunks. With strangers. With the kind of volatile men who existed only in the late-night haze of downtown saloons. It was a training ground for something larger—endurance. And beneath it all, he began to understand the shape of urban Native life.

The difference between reservation Indians and urban Indians was stark. On the reservation, even in poverty, there was nature—hunting, fishing, ricing, forest walks, canoeing. A connection to land and rhythm. But in the city, that life vanished. Urban Indians lived in brick buildings and tattered housing, often surrounded by hostility, squeezed by stereotypes, and getting little in return. The phrase "concrete jungle" wasn't just metaphor. It was memoir.

In that jungle, the old ways were harder to live. But Leonard never let them go. He carried them silently, watching how his People adapted, stumbled, survived.

The Silent Preparation

By fourteen, Leonard Prescott had become a paradox—part boy, part guardian, part witness to a household splintered by pain. He bore no badge, carried no weapon, and raised no voice. Yet among his siblings, he was the one who stayed. He was the one who endured.

The others had scattered in search of something more solid—some future outside of Saint Paul's narrow alleyways and rented apartments. But Leonard remained because they asked him to. "You can't run away, Leonard," they'd say. "You're our example." That word stuck with him—"example." Not hero. Not savior. Just a quiet standard-bearer for a family weathering the tailwinds of historical violence and modern poverty.

He didn't talk much about what he saw. The drunken fights. The belt in the attic. The hunger that made a boy steal from his mother's purse. The way his mother disappeared inside herself when the world became too loud. These weren't events. They were rhythms—an unspoken score that shaped how he moved through the world.

Instead, he trained. With no gym, no mentor, and no roadmap, he built his own discipline. He pushed his body until it stopped feeling fragile. He used boards, then bricks, then walls, transforming soft knuckles into silent declarations—*I am not helpless. I am not afraid. I am not running.*

Yet there was more than just the physical.

His brother Alan had given him stories—not just of fights, but of structure, routine, brotherhood. In the strange way of institutional life, Totem Town, a juvenile detention center in Battle Creek, Minnesota, had become a place of both punishment and clarity. Leonard envied that, even though he dreaded what it represented. He didn't want prison bars. He didn't want guards. But he wanted to be tested. To know he could endure.

So he built his tests in silence.

And as the city shifted around him—as landlords changed, neighborhoods gentrified, and the scars of old battles faded into new ones—Leonard carried something that didn't change. He carried a sense that the world was broken but could be repaired. That injustice was not an accident but a structure. And that survival, though necessary, was not enough.

Somewhere in that quiet furnace of hardship and shame, Leonard began to kindle the first sparks of something larger. He didn't yet have the words for it. But it would come to be known later as service. As organizing. As… sovereignty.

For now, he was the older brother. The one who stayed. The one who listened. The one who learned that strength wasn't just fists or endurance. It was knowing when to walk away. It was knowing when to stay home. It was knowing how not to be swallowed by the streets, or the bottle, or the inherited sorrow passed down like an heirloom from men who'd seen too much and said too little.

The world hadn't yet made room for an Indian boy from Morton to rise in politics or to speak at national gatherings. But Leonard was already rising—inwardly, slowly, like a tree taking root beneath cracked pavement.

He wasn't trying to be a leader.

He was trying to be whole.

Leonard's siblings began peeling away. All of them ran away at some point, searching for stability elsewhere. Alan, the brother closest in age, turned to petty crime by breaking into parking meters and stealing from department stores. Eventually, the authorities caught him, and he was sent to Boys Totem Town.

Leonard and the family would visit him. Alan, wearing ragged shoes marked BTT, would sometimes be found scrubbing the floors with steel wool, forced to polish away the scuff marks left by other visitors. It was a punishment—not for dirt, but for insubordination, for fighting, for talking back.

Still, Alan didn't stay there. He escaped. More than once.

One day, Leonard saw him downtown while selling newspapers on a street corner. Alan had gained weight, some of it muscle. He looked tougher—torn clothes, close-shaved head, eyes sharper than before. Leonard barely recognized him. Alan needed money, food, something clean to wear. But more than that, he needed someone to listen.

He told Leonard about life inside—the rivalries, the fights, the makeshift sports. They played football, basketball, bucket ball—a violent mash of competition where scores could be settled through physical domination. If you had a grudge, you could resolve it in the boxing ring. If you didn't, the ring might still find you.

Leonard listened like he was hearing a war story. There was honor in it, danger, identity. A kind of strength that Leonard admired and craved.

At night, the two brothers would lie in their shared room. Alan would tell stories. Push-ups, sit-ups, knuckle drills. Wrestling moves. Street wisdom. Escape routes. Leonard drank in every word.

He began his own training—first in secret, then in ritual. Push-ups on the floor. Sit-ups. Then punching—small boards at first, then bigger ones. Eventually, concrete walls. He did it until the pain stopped. Until his fists felt like stone.

He didn't want to fight. Not exactly. But he wanted to be ready. In a city where violence prowled every corner, readiness was survival.

His quiet demeanor, his watchful eyes, and now his growing strength gave him a presence. Alan's friends respected him and called him "the older brother." Others left him alone.

Leonard had no formal training in self-defense. But he had discipline, and discipline became his armor. He wasn't learning to hurt others. He was learning not to be hurt.

He returned to Saint Paul before the school year ended, back to the West Side, back to the Mexican-American neighborhoods he'd known before. But things had changed. The streets were shifting. Tensions rose like storm clouds.

Street Tensions and Survival

Across the country, equality struggles were shaking the foundations of cities, and in neighborhoods like Selby-Dale, those questions of "how far does equality really go?" were answered with fists, knives, and the occasional gunshot.

One night, a party at Dundeen turned deadly. A Black man arrived, tempers flared, and a knife appeared in the chaos. He fled out the door and down the street, pursued by a pack of young men. When they caught him, the stabbing was merciless—wounds all over his body. He died.

In the aftermath, parents in the neighborhood worried that the killing would spark retaliation from the Black families nearby. As racial tensions escalated through the late '60s, the divide between Black and Mexican neighborhoods sharpened. Threats were exchanged. Territory lines hardened.

For two or three nights after the stabbing, Leonard and a group of his friends patrolled the corners around their neighborhood, carrying whatever weapons they could find—shotguns, .22 rifles, handguns lifted from their parents' closets or stolen from somewhere else. They saw themselves as "protectors," convinced they were safeguarding their families if retaliation came. It never did. After a few tense evenings, they stood down. But the readiness remained.

The Latin Counts, a street gang with increasing influence in the neighborhood, had begun asserting their presence. Their members—mostly older teens—had swagger, sharp clothes, and a reputation for violence. Leonard, still a high school student but built with muscle from years of training, found himself in their sights.

It started small. A sideways glance. A whispered insult. A friend warning him not to walk a certain block. Then one day, it wasn't a warning. Leonard and his brother, Robbie, were shooting pool at Harkin's Pool Hall when one of the bigger Counts pushed up against Leonard and gruffly said, "I need two bucks." Clearly, a demand. Leonard glanced at the Count and said, "Wait till I finish," a potentially dangerous response. To Leonard's recollection, he played the best game of his life, perhaps because the adrenalin was flowing.

"Gimme two bucks now," the Count said when the game concluded, but Leonard sternly said, "No." The Count angrily nodded for Leonard to follow him up the stairs, which he did, with Robbie following. "Whatever you do, don't run," Leonard whispered to his brother. Somehow, Leonard managed to settle down his adversary without violence, a small show of mutual respect.

In that moment, he understood something essential—violence was a language, and in certain neighborhoods, fluency in that language meant survival. But real power—lasting power—came from knowing when to speak it and when to walk away.

He continued to walk freely, head high, fists loose. And though trouble still lurked, it no longer hunted him. He had earned space—not just through strength, but through presence.

Angie

In ninth grade, at the Humboldt School back in Saint Paul, Leonard met a girl who would have a great impact on him later in life. Angie Longoria was a good friend of Leonard's sisters. "She was a good friend to them," Leonard told me in an interview. "She would do just about anything for them, but at that young age, I wasn't interested in any kind of relationship with a girl."

In tenth grade, Angie was still at Humboldt with Leonard, and he actively tried to avoid her. "I was pretty cold to her, actually," Leonard remembered. "By the eleventh grade, Angie and her family moved to Texas, and she eventually got married down there." But that would not be the end of it.

Seeing Connections

Leonard Prescott had always carried weight beyond his years—first as the eldest son in a turbulent home, then as a quiet survivor of the city's unrelenting streets. At Humboldt High School on the West Side of Saint Paul, he couldn't help noticing the student body was a mix of working-class White kids, Mexican-Americans, and a growing number of Native students, many of whom had migrated from reservations during the era of federal relocation and termination policies. There were no courses in Tribal history, no Indigenous language classes, no Native counselors.

Nevertheless, Leonard began to piece together something that had always existed inside him but never had a name—the political shape of injustice. It wasn't just that his family had moved constantly. It wasn't just that there had been hunger, violence, and silence. It was that all these things were connected—to broken treaties, to indifferent school systems, to housing policies that herded families into cheap, drafty buildings without support.

He began to ask questions—not only about his own family, but about why so many Native kids ended up in juvenile detention. Why alcoholism hollowed out the lives of uncles and cousins. Why the police treated his friends differently. Why teachers assumed he wouldn't graduate.

The answers didn't come all at once. But the questions never left.

Outside school, Leonard kept his discipline. He still trained his body—push-ups, knuckle drills, silent challenges made visible only in the bruises. He had no mentors, but he read people like books. He watched how adults moved through power. He listened to the way men boasted in bars and the way women carried strength in their silence. He noticed how some folks bowed their heads in shame when the word "Indian" was spoken, and others straightened their backs.

He began to straighten his.

He wasn't organizing protests. He wasn't giving speeches. But when there was conflict between students, Leonard was the one others asked to mediate. When a teacher made a careless comment about Native People, it was Leonard who raised his hand—not with anger, but with calm certainty. "That's not accurate," he'd say. "Here's what really happened."

At home, things were still fragile. His mother worked constantly. His father drifted in and out of contact. His siblings pursued their own paths. But Leonard stayed steady. He became a kind of quiet hinge in the family—a bridge between generations, a listener when others shouted, a protector when others fled.

At night, when the streets fell quiet and the bars closed down, Leonard would sometimes walk the neighborhood, hands in his pockets, eyes scanning the sky. He didn't know what he was looking for exactly. But something called to him—an urgency, a responsibility not yet fully born.

The United Soul

As a teenager, Leonard watched the neighborhood continue to change. By eleventh grade at Humboldt High School, most of his free time was with the United Soul—an association not well regarded by his mostly White classmates. The West Side had three main groups. The Brown Berets, an offshoot of the Latin Counts, were Mexican-American activists pushing for social change. The Chicano United were also Mexican-American, more mischievous and less politically driven. The United Souls were broader—activists who accepted anyone: Black, White, Indian, Mexican-American.

Tensions weren't rare. Late in the school year, words between some Mexican-American members of United Soul and the White senior class escalated into name-calling and slurs. The leaders agreed to settle things the way young men often did—face-to-face, at the Humboldt High football field, nine p.m. on a Thursday.

United Soul arrived early, spread out across the field, waiting. Leonard's thoughts kept circling: *This is really going to happen.* When the seniors arrived, they came in cars, screeching to a halt, piling out with baseball bats, beer bottles, and other weapons.

Schmitty, one of the Soul—not a tough guy—stepped forward to speak. Before he got a sentence out, someone smashed a beer bottle over his head. He went down, and fists clenched all around. But before the first charge, sirens split the night. Police swarmed in from every direction, and the crowd scattered. The fight never happened.

Walking home with a smaller group, a carload of seniors pulled alongside, jeering. We challenged them; they drove off. The next day at school, they kept their distance. The confrontation had run its course. Like boxers after a final bell, each side returned to its corner. Leonard was left an outsider—no longer a target, but never fully one of them.

Attempted Robbery

One night, Leonard was arrested for his role in an attempted robbery. It was the result of a chaotic, drunken night when a friend tightened a rope around a man's neck and everyone else ran. Leonard stayed. Not out of violence, but loyalty to his community. It cost him. He was caught and pled guilty to get his friend off the hook. With no prior record, he got probation. The conviction was eventually reduced to a misdemeanor and was expunged, but it followed him—lingering like smoke in the eyes of future accusers.

Looking for a Place to Belong

Gymnastics had been his anchor since seventh grade—parallel bars, free exercise, occasional turns on the high bar or trampoline. It gave him discipline and the satisfaction of building skill. He wasn't a good student—a C average at best—but he became the first in his family to graduate.

Graduation day was anticlimactic. The class was dismissed around ten thirty a.m., and Leonard walked home alone, a strange relief settling in. High school had been more endurance test than celebration. On the way, a brand-new '69 Camaro roared past, filled with White kids hanging out the windows, shouting in triumph about their futures. He watched the car vanish and wondered how kids his age could afford such a thing.

At school, those same kids spoke casually of vacations to Florida or California. Leonard's reality was smaller. No job. No money. No parents with money. The farthest he could imagine traveling was the Wisconsin Dells—and even that was someday.

Unexpected Doors

A Classroom in Survival

Leonard's youth in Saint Paul unfolded against a backdrop of turbulence that seemed to set the entire country on fire. The United Soul, the gang he had helped to form, was more than a circle of friends—it was a crucible for identity. They stood at the edge of Black neighborhoods, Mexican neighborhoods, and White working-class enclaves, watching tensions mount.

For Leonard, the West Side streets became a classroom in survival and solidarity. He learned that injustice was not confined to one community. African-Americans, Mexican-Americans, and Indians all bore its weight. He watched as the Black Panthers rose in power, boldly resisting police violence, and he saw Mexican-American groups like the Brown Berets press their cause with equal fire. On Franklin Avenue in Minneapolis, a new Indian voice began to rise. Russell Means, George Mitchell, Dennis Banks, Clyde Bellecourt, and others were setting in motion what soon became the American Indian Movement—AIM—a force that would forever change the landscape of Native activism.

Leonard recognized the same undercurrent in his own circle. The United Soul was born of a need for protection, but it carried within it the same demand AIM was voicing—recognition, dignity, sovereignty. What AIM made national, Leonard and his friends felt in their bones every time they walked their block with shotguns and .22 rifles after a killing, promising their parents and neighbors they would not let the violence come unchallenged.

The wider world pressed in. The Vietnam War had spread like a stain across Leonard's generation. Draft notices went out, and protests followed. Students for a Democratic Society—known in his neighborhood simply as SDS, though sometimes called "SOS"—marched in the streets, handing out flyers, preaching against war abroad and injustice at home. They weren't content to chant. They brought paralegals to defend against unlawful arrests, demanded better health care for minority communities, and urged citizens to storm city council meetings with their grievances. To Leonard, they looked like allies. To the authorities, they were dangerous radicals.

And then came the hippies. Tens of thousands gathered under banners of peace, waving placards that read "Make Love, Not War." They filled parks with song, talk of justice, and haze from marijuana and stronger drugs—LSD, cocaine, heroin—that bled into neighborhoods already straining under poverty. Leonard could feel the pull of their movement, the promise of freedom, even as he saw the destruction drugs left in their wake.

All these currents met in him—the United Soul, AIM, SDS, hippies, radicals, Panthers, Brown Berets. "Great change begins with great diversity," he would later say, and in those days he was living diversity in its rawest form. He didn't need textbooks. The streets, the protests, the violence, and the solidarity of marginalized people became his education.

Work, NSP, and Hard Lessons

In the midst of upheaval, Leonard worked. The Post Office gave him his first steady paycheck. He delivered mail and sorted stacks in cavernous rooms, a cog in the federal machine. Later, he moved into the foundry, where smoke and heat wrapped around him, where steel clanged until his ears rang. The work was harsh, but it was honest, and it left its mark.

For a time, he found work as a pipe-fitter at Northern States Power, a company that seemed at first to offer stability. But Leonard quickly saw another face of corporate America. Indians were not welcomed into management or trained for advancement. Instead, they were kept on the margins. NSP, like so many others, claimed to serve the public while profiting from it, keeping minorities out of decision-making roles. To Leonard, it was another lesson in how power operated: carefully guarding itself, offering wages but not respect, labor but not leadership.

These jobs kept him alive, but they didn't satisfy. The question burned: *Is this all my life will be? A laborer on someone else's terms?*

Laura Singer and the Door to College

One day, without plan or preparation, Leonard walked into an employment agency. The woman behind the desk, Laura Singer, surprised him. She didn't just take his name and hand him a form. She looked at him—really studied him—and asked questions about what he liked, what he was capable of, what he wanted his life to mean.

Laura spoke of possibilities Leonard had never dared imagine. She told him about the University of Minnesota's General College, a place where students like him could start, build credits, then transfer into the College of Liberal Arts. From there, he could choose a major, maybe even become a high school coach.

The suggestion left Leonard stunned. College was something other people did—White kids with money, kids who weren't marked by gangs, poverty, or Indian identity. But Laura insisted.

The thought of college was flattering. Leonard loved exercise, gymnastics, the training of the body. The idea of teaching it, of guiding young people, appealed to him deeply. *Me? In college*? he wondered. The tantalizing idea felt impossibly distant. He wasn't ready—not yet. The streets still had lessons to teach, and the horizon of Indian politics was only beginning to reveal itself to him.

But Laura had planted the seed. And eventually Leonard watered it. He became the first in his family to attend college, enrolling at the University of Minnesota. There, he found himself gravitating not toward Indian student groups—his own culture had been stripped too far from him—but toward Mexican-American peers. With them he felt a kind of kinship, a recognition born of shared marginalization. They were active, committed, challenging injustice in their own way. Surrounded by them, Leonard felt a sense of belonging that Indian identity alone had not yet given him.

Summers with Northern States Power

During the summers between college semesters, Leonard found steady work at Northern States Power. They placed him in the natural gas department, first as a laborer, then as an apprentice pipefitter. He was hired under the company's "Minority Advocacy" program, which was supposed to expand opportunity for underrepresented workers. Yet when Leonard arrived, he found only two other minority men on the entire workforce: Bob Cruz and Cecil Hernandez. The job itself was grueling but straightforward. Crews dug into city streets, hauling out corroded cast-iron gas mains and replacing them with newly developed polyethylene plastic piping.

The following summer, Leonard applied again under the same program. This time NSP turned him down, claiming the minority status only applied to the first year. Leonard knew better. The company had hired only two minority workers in total, and their explanation rang hollow. He decided not to accept "No" for an answer.

Leonard went to the St. Paul Human Rights Agency and filed a complaint. Within weeks, Human Rights sent a letter to NSP questioning the practice. Two weeks later, the company reversed itself. Leonard was rehired, this time as a full-time apprentice pipefitter.

It was his first direct encounter with discrimination, and also his first victory against it. "It was the first time I had felt discriminated against and yet came out with a positive outcome," Leonard told me. For him, the lesson was clear—sometimes the only way forward was to challenge the system head-on. He stayed with Northern States Power for the next seven years.

Love and the Mount Airy Projects

Those years at NSP overlapped with another defining turn in Leonard's life. He crossed paths again with Linda Robledo, a Mexican-American woman he had first noticed years earlier. He remembered her as a feisty eighth-grader when he was in tenth—sharp-eyed, confident, always quick to push back against anyone who tried to impose on her. When they met again Leonard was twenty, and Linda was no longer the carefree girl he remembered. She had been married, had a child, and was newly divorced.

Leonard was drawn to her immediately. Infatuation swept through him with a force he could not resist. "She was the first love of my life," he later said. Linda was working at a Target store in West St. Paul, not far from where her ex-husband still lived. Their courtship moved quickly. Before long Leonard had moved in with her, her young daughter Dedi, and Linda's mother in the Mount Airy

Projects near the state capitol. For the first time in his life, Leonard was living away from his mother and brothers.

The relationship was complicated from the beginning. Trust issues flared, and the two had no shared vision for what their future should be. Still, when their daughter Denise was born, Leonard was overjoyed. He felt proud of the growing family that now included Linda, Dedi, and Denise. They shared many firsts—visits to restaurants, trips to the zoo, simple outings that Leonard had never experienced in his own childhood. In those moments, life felt good.

But beneath the surface, problems stirred. Alcohol was part of both their lives, and it fueled conflicts that neither could resolve. Leonard recognized it as a co-dependent relationship, one that pulled both of them deeper into drinking.

Pipefitters and the Culture of Alcohol

At work, Leonard took pride in his performance. He did his job well and earned the respect of the crews. But the construction culture of the 1970s was steeped in alcohol. Among the pipefitters at NSP, the mark of toughness wasn't only in the work done underground, but in the ability to hold liquor aboveground.

Mornings often began with a trip to the coffee shop—unless, as sometimes happened, a few men decided to detour to the bar. Lunchtime frequently meant sandwiches with beer chasers. On hot afternoons, the thought of digging trenches and locating gas pipes while under the influence seemed absurd to Leonard, yet it was part of the rhythm of the job. Supervisors set the tone. Some would step outside, feel a drop of rain, and declare, "Let's wait it out and go to the bar." Others ignored even heavy downpours and kept their men working. Depending on which crew Leonard was assigned to, the level of alcohol exposure in a single day could vary dramatically.

"I don't know that I would claim the title of 'alcoholic,'" Leonard told me, "but I did follow the cultural norms of the industry at the time."

Fractures at Home

Even as Leonard longed for stability, Linda's priorities ran in another direction. She loved the nightlife—bars, clubs, evenings out with friends—and sought excitement and independence. Their lifestyles diverged, and Leonard began to dislike the person he was becoming. He knew he would have to change if he wanted a different life.

NSP began to notice the toll as well. Leonard started showing up late, missing days, or slipping in and out of stretches of reliability. By his fourth year, management confronted him. They told him he had been given enough chances. If he wanted to keep his job, he would have to enter alcohol treatment.

Leonard agreed.

St. Joseph's Hospital

He enrolled in a thirty-day rehabilitation program at St. Joseph's Hospital in downtown St. Paul. The experience forced him to confront the role alcohol had played in his life. "What I got out of the program," he said, "was a sense of whether I was really in control. What was alcohol doing in my life?"

He came to believe that the problem was not only the drinking itself but the environment surrounding it—the alcohol-heavy culture of construction work and the instability at home with Linda. He learned that alcohol crossed the line into true danger when it led to missed days, broken obligations, or a breakdown of family relationships. At that point, it was no longer a habit—it was a problem.

The program sharpened his priorities. It gave him clarity about what he wanted his life to be. Part of the treatment plan required spouses to join in addressing alcohol use. Leonard tried to bring Linda into that process, hoping they could both change, but she refused. In her view, Leonard was the one with the problem. She continued to live as she pleased.

Their relationship drifted on and off, alcohol always part of the equation. Eventually, it eroded Leonard's standing at NSP as well. Eventually, he was terminated and returned once again to the employment office in search of work.

Three months passed after losing his job. Unemployment was a bitter education in itself, but once again it was Laura Singer who opened a door for him. Through her assistance, he was hired full-time at Naegele Outdoor Advertising, a company known for its sprawling billboards across the Twin Cities.

The work was different from anything he had done before. There was a touch of creativity in it—metal, construction, design—all tied to the massive structures that dotted highways and city streets. Leonard joined the Sheet Metal Workers Union, and in his last year at Naegele he achieved journeyman status, a point of pride after years of shifting jobs. He managed to build a steady rhythm of employment that had eluded him before.

During that time, his relationship with Linda Robledo came to a permanent end. They had never been married, but the years of living together, the raising of Denise, and the long cycle of conflict had bound them in ways that separation could not erase overnight. Still, by the mid-1970s it was finished. Leonard knew it was time to let go.

In 1973, he made a decision that would alter the trajectory of his life. He moved back onto the Shakopee reservation, returning to the house where his mother still lived. "Mom always had an open door for her children," Leonard remembered, "and I very happily went home."

It was a return not only to family but to identity. The reservation had changed since his youth, yet it still bore the weight of generations struggling with the same fundamental questions— how to govern themselves, how to survive, how to prosper in a society that had tried to erase them.

Fatherhood

Fatherhood should have anchored him, but instead it helped expose the fractures in his life. The pressures of an ill-matched marriage, the responsibilities of child-rearing, and the restless desire to do something meaningful with his life proved too much. Leonard found himself unable to reconcile all of it—work, school, family, identity. The relationship unraveled quickly.

When it ended, Leonard felt uprooted, stripped of direction. He moved to the reservation at Shakopee, carrying with him both the weight of fatherhood and the emptiness of loss. It was a turning point, though he did not yet know it. On the reservation, new lessons awaited—lessons about sovereignty, self-sufficiency, and the fragility of community.

Rose Blossom's House

Leonard Prescott's identity, like that of his People, was forged in a landscape of contested truths. At the heart of his life story lay a question that had haunted the community for generations: Who truly belonged?

His mother, Rose Blossom, came from the Santee People—Dakota who had been exiled from Minnesota after the US–Dakota War of 1862 and forced to rebuild lives far from ancestral lands. Yet Rose's bloodline, her memory, and her resilience rooted Leonard in Shakopee. She was among those who had returned after the exile, whose presence formed the bridge between dispossession and survival. She had supported Norman M. Crooks, Leonard's uncle and one of the key figures in establishing the modern reservation. In doing so, she became one of the founding members of what would become the Shakopee Mdewakanton Sioux Community (SMSC).

Her presence granted Leonard more than heritage—it granted legitimacy. The right to vote. The right to hold land. The right to speak. These rights were not abstract. They were embedded in federal recognition, in the treaty of 1851, and in the often-contested 1886 roll, the list that formed the basis of enrollment for the Mdewakanton People. Eventually, Leonard would study that roll closely, understand its profound implications, and watch in later years as its integrity became blurred.

Rose Blossom Prescott's house on the reservation.

Rose Blossom owned a house on the reservation, and in 1972, after his relationship with Linda Robledo disintegrated, Leonard moved into that house with his mother. But then, Norman Crooks, who was married to her sister, turned on Rose Blossom and decided to disenroll her from the community on the grounds that she was enrolled as a Santee, thus ineligible for enrollment as a Mdewakanton

Sioux. And further, Norm claimed, Rose did not have lineage back to the 1886 Treaty, which only allowed enrollment of direct descendants of "qualified" Indians. Never mind that Norm was also a Santee. Under a handshake proposition from Norm—perhaps a "family discount"—Rose was still allowed to vote in community elections, a perplexing paradox.Because Leonard's father provided him with undisputed lineage back to the 1886 requirements for enrollment, Rose suggested that she give her brand new house, which she now had to vacate, to her eldest son. After all, Leonard had never lived in a truly settled home. His clothes were scattered between his sister's place, his father's house, and other borrowed corners.

"The first thing I thought was, *I don't think so*," Leonard told me. "This reservation was like in the middle of nowhere. And I was used to living in the exciting city where there were so many things to do. The rez was all dirt roads. There wasn't a paved road in sight. But Mom didn't have anyone in the family she could give it to. The other family members already had homes. I was old enough to have one now, so she convinced me that I should take the house. The refinancing was only going to be about $19,000, and I think she bought it for $40,000. My monthly payment would be only eighty-two dollars a month for the next thirty years. I had a car, so I could get back to the west side of Saint Paul if I wanted to. So I took over the house and lived permanently on the reservation in 1975."

The Epiphany

At Naegele, Leonard worked alongside Michael Dehealy, a co-worker whose interest in social and political questions matched his own. Day after day, week after week, their conversations circled back to the same themes—the early struggles of the Shakopee Sioux Indian Community (SMSC). They spoke about housing shortages, the gaps in health care, the inadequacy of education, and the scarcity of decent jobs.

Finally, after one of these conversations, Michael turned to him and said, "Leonard, why don't you just run for the business council and become a part of it?"

The suggestion startled Leonard. He had not thought of himself as a political figure, nor had he developed the instincts of an executive or the polish of a businessman. Yet Michael's words planted a seed. Something in Leonard's life was about to change. More than one thing, in fact.

Angi Redux

The other new direction for Leonard occurred when Angie Longoria reappeared in Minnesota freshly divorced. With new eyes, Leonard found this girl, whom he had once treated so shabbily, very appealing.

"She was deeply involved with religion then—a Jehovah's Witness, earnest and grounded," Leonard told me. He thought perhaps that was what he needed. At first, theirs was not a physical relationship; he believed staying away from that would give the relationship more stability. But Angie began weaving God's teachings into their connection, convincing him that closeness, even sexual relations, was not wrong if it came from a true bond. He went along, and later they had a child together—David.

But Angie herself was restless. She was searching for something she couldn't name. Often she felt she didn't belong to this world, convinced she was born into the wrong generation. She saw immorality everywhere, and it weighed on her. She smoked marijuana constantly. Leonard did not, but he saw how it lifted her spirits—and how, when the smoke cleared, she fell into deep depressions.

Leonard and Angie were married on the reservation and moved into Rose Blossom's house, but the household lived on the edge of her moods. Sometimes she erupted in anger while Leonard tried to stay calm, listening while she repeated the same grievances again and again. Once, in a fit of fury, she smashed an entire curio set onto the floor. Leonard only told her, flatly, that he wouldn't be the one to clean it up. Other times, after an emotional storm, she would abruptly leave, walking down the freeway, prophetically threatening suicide.

Leonard would pile the children—Denise, David and Angie's son from her previous marriage, who were already too used to these scenes—into his van and drive after her. He remembered one evening when the kids, sitting in front of *Little House on the Prairie*, asked almost casually, "When is it going to be your turn?" They were only children, but the chaos had become routine. Leonard would pull up beside Angie on the freeway, coaxing: "Come on, Angie, get into the truck. Let's just talk." Eventually she would climb in, the immediate crisis passed, though never fully resolved.

The cycle always returned. While she was never officially diagnosed with bipolar disorder, her behavior closely resembled it.

At night, sleep was elusive. Every sound set him on edge. Angie's rage could cut so sharply that he sometimes lay awake wondering, *Will I be stabbed tonight?* Still, he didn't leave. He told himself, *You can't just leave. No matter what, you can't leave her like this.* And so he endured. Through it all, he stayed, trying to work through the storms, tethered by family, by loyalty, and by a determination to face what came.

The turmoil of life with Angie, for all its exhaustion and danger, also forced Leonard to turn his gaze outward. At home he lived with constant unpredictability—moods that swung from devotion to destruction, from desperate searching to despair. There were no clear answers, no mentors to guide him, and no precedent for how to navigate the storms. In a way, that mirrored what he saw in his community. If survival in his marriage meant holding steady in chaos, then survival for his People meant the same—finding a path through confusion and conflict without anyone to show him the way forward.

The stresses at home sharpened his sense that his private struggles were part of a larger pattern. Indian communities across Minnesota—and beyond—were facing crises of their own—sovereignty in name but not in practice, dependence where there should have been self-sufficiency, and bitter feuding that weakened every attempt at progress. Few in the community had experience in organizing or administering affairs. They were like Leonard himself—untrained, unguided, disconnected from the cultural anchors that had once given strength, cut off from the wider world that might have offered models to learn from.

Out of necessity, Leonard began to see beyond his household. Personal survival and community survival were twined together. If he could endure and search for solutions at home, then he could also imagine new ways forward for a People still finding their place between sovereignty and survival.

And then, suddenly, after a few years of restless existence, Angie was gone.

One day she called Leonard, her voice steady, almost calm. They talked about her getting help, about finally seeing a psychologist.

"Yeah," she told him, "I was thinking about that psychologist, and I want to go. I'm going to do that." For a moment, Leonard felt a glimmer of relief. But then Angie said, "Excuse me, could you hold the phone just a minute…?" The line fell silent. Suddenly, Leonard heard a gunshot… then the girls—still teenagers, barely fourteen—coming into the room, their voices rising in panic. He knew something terrible had happened.

At work, his unease grew. He asked his friend Sally Milroy, who knew Angie well, to phone the house or ask the Welches, neighbors across the street, to check on his wife. Soon word came back that the children were screaming outside in the yard.

Leonard rushed home. On his way, he crossed paths with Angie's son from her earlier marriage, who worked at the warehouse. The boy's grief-stricken expression told Leonard the truth before he reached the house. Angie had shot herself.

Leonard sat numbly on the couch, unable to go into the room where her body lay. He couldn't bring himself to look. When they carried her out in a body bag, his head throbbed with disbelief.

Angie's family turned on him in their grief, asking, "What did you do? What did you do to her?" He had no answer, but the questions haunted him. He hadn't done anything. But maybe that meant he hadn't done enough. That was the ache of it.

The children, though, were not surprised. They had grown up with Angie's swings between tenderness and rage, her walks down the freeway threatening to end her life, her marijuana highs followed by deep plunges into despair. Leonard remembered other moments too—like the time he had broken down a door to find her clutching razor blades, her eyes wide with shame as she whispered, "I'm so sorry." On that occasion, he had kept his voice calm, telling her they didn't need to stay married, that she didn't need to feel guilty, that they could simply talk. She put the blades down at last, but Leonard knew how close he had come to losing her even then. If he had entered the room just seconds later, he thought, it might have been different.

Her death left scars that never fully faded. For Leonard, it was more than grief. It was a brutal reminder of how fragile a life could be without balance, guidance or hope. Even before Angie's death, he had begun to recognize the same absence in his community. Like Angie, Indian communities across the state carried wounds with no clear remedy. Indians were largely disconnected from their own traditions, isolated from the larger society, untrained in the skills of organizing or governance, divided by old feuds and unmet needs. Even Angie's unhappy life had been awakening Leonard to the realization that to survive, his Mdewakanton community would have to find what his wife could not—a way to heal, to steady itself, to envision a future.

That awakening would deepen as he settled more fully into life on the reservation. His private sorrows slowly transformed into determination, driving him toward the work of sovereignty, self-sufficiency, and leadership. Out of personal tragedy, he turned to face the collective challenges of his People, believing that somewhere in the struggle lay the path to wholeness. "It was an extraordinary experienced to befriend my reservation family," he explained.

Integrity as Survival

For Leonard, the struggle over enrollment was not abstract. It began at his own family's door. His mother, Rose Blossom Prescott, had been suddenly told she did not qualify as a member of the Shakopee Mdewakanton Sioux Community. Norman Crooks, Leonard's uncle, argued that Rose was not descended from the 1886 "friendlies" and was instead enrolled as Santee. The Bureau of Indian Affairs (BIA) agreed, ordering her to vacate her house on reservation land. The message was stark—unless someone in the family could prove 1886 status, she would be forced out.

That's when Leonard stepped in to gain ownership of his mother's house. His father's family held 1886 recognition from Morton, and Leonard was able to claim the house under that authority. But the ordeal left him shaken. Why could his mother be cast aside on such contested grounds while others—like Norman M. Crooks himself—retained membership despite Santee enrollment? He later recalled that some of the original thirteen charter members, Crooks included, had been simply included without proving ancestry, a shortcut that haunted the tribe's integrity. And on the sign-in register, it appears that the signatures of these charter members were all written in the same handwriting.

REGISTER OF VOTERS

Election of November 4, 1969

1. Edith Crooks
2. Rosema Crooks
3. Norman M. Crooks
4. Anne L Crooks
5. Lanny A. Ross
6. Mamie Grofas
7. Norman W. Crooks
8. Raymond B. Crooks
9. Ernest Raymon Emerson
10. John Cermak
11. Edward Cermack
12. [illegible] Brewer
13. Linda Brewer

The register of voters for the Nov. 4, 1969 election. Note that all signatures appear to have been written by the same hand.

This was Leonard's awakening. Membership was not just paperwork, it was survival. If rules could be bent or ignored, families like his could lose everything. From then on, he and his sister Pat immersed themselves in the old rolls, tracing names and categories back to 1886 and gaining a deep appreciation for the importance of established rules and regulations.

He learned that the 1886 rolls are at the heart of the Shakopee Mdewakanton Sioux Community's (SMSC) identity and membership debates. They were created by federal authorities as part of the aftermath of the US-Dakota War of 1862 and the subsequent exile of most Dakota People from Minnesota.

Leonard Prescott with his mother, Rose Blossom Prescott.

The 1886 Rolls

In 1886, the US government authorized a census-like enrollment of Dakota People who were considered "loyal Mdewakanton" or "friendlies." These were families who had not joined the 1862 uprising against the federal government or settlers—or in some cases, those who had actively aided White settlers. Because of this "loyalty," they were permitted to remain in Minnesota when most Dakota were expelled.

The 1886 rolls (sometimes called the *1886 U.S. Indian Census Rolls* or the *1886 Mdewakanton Sioux rolls*) were not a single tidy list, but a set of federal rosters created to identify the "loyal Mdewakanton" and their descendants who were allowed to remain in Minnesota after 1862. The three main rolls connected to the "friendly" Mdewakanton were:

- **1886 McLeod Roll** compiled by U.S. Special Agent Walter McLeod. It is sometimes called the *McLeod Census* or *McLeod Roll.* It listed the "loyal Mdewakanton" families living near Shakopee, Prior Lake, and Mendota. This roll later became central for enrollment disputes in the Shakopee Mdewakanton Sioux Community (SMSC).

- **1886 Henton Roll** compiled by Agent Henton. This roll covered "loyal Mdewakanton" living in other areas, including around Morton and Redwood Falls.

- **1886 Campbell Roll** compiled by Agent Campbell. This roll focused on groups living in the lower Minnesota River valley near Redwood Agency.

The governing documents, as Leonard studied them, spelled out three categories of membership:

- base roll members whose specific names appeared in one of the original rolls

- children of enrolled members, provided they carried at least ¼ Indian blood

- descendants of certain Mdewakanton Sioux, again with ¼ blood and other qualifications

The Formation of the SMSC Constitution

Before the adoption of the 1969 Constitution, Leonard's mother was drawn into discussions that would shape the destiny of Shakopee. Edith, her sister, urged her to attend the early gatherings—informal round-table meetings of Mdewakanton descendants exploring whether they could form a new community. Edith and Norman

Crooks both understood something crucial—the Prescott family had authentic proof of descent. Their lineage tied them back to those who had not joined the 1862 uprising, a qualification that carried weight not just in memory but in law.

Crooks knew that proof mattered. For the new community to receive recognition and benefits from the Bureau of Indian Affairs, members would have to trace their ancestry to the 1886 rolls.

A few other families living on Shakopee land held the same legitimacy. Mamie Goofas, John Cermack, Lois Brewer, and Elizabeth "Babe" Vig were among them. Their ties to the 1886 lists were well documented.

But in those years the Shakopee lands were bare. There were no sewers, no running water, no infrastructure. Life there offered little but the sovereign status of the land itself. That status, however, meant freedom from state and federal taxes and, more than that, a sense of connection to Dakota history. To live on trust land was to feel tethered to an identity that outsiders had tried to erase.

Crooks quickly grasped how powerful this was. Many people wanted in. The lure of sovereignty, combined with the convenience of living near the growing Twin Cities—with its schools, hospitals, and jobs—made membership attractive. He contacted as many as forty-two people as potential members. But whether all of them were qualified would never be decided. An event engineered by Crooks would cut the list down to thirteen charter members whose names alone would appear in the Constitution.

Articles of Membership

Crooks himself could not trace ancestry to the 1886 rolls. He devised a path forward anyway. The Constitution's first article enshrined the charter members as beneficiaries, exempting them from scrutiny. The second article allowed their children membership, provided they could prove one-quarter Mdewakanton Sioux blood and descent from the 1886 lists. The third article set the same requirements for any future applicants, who would also have to reside on Shakopee land. Here is the exact language extracted directly from that constitution:

> Article II – MEMBERSHIP, Section 1
>
> (a) All persons of Mdewakanton Sioux Indian blood, not members of any other Indian tribe, band or group, whose names appear on the 1969 census roll of Mdewakanton Sioux residents of the Prior Lake Reservation, Minnesota, prepared specifically for the purpose of organizing the Shakopee Mdewakanton Sioux Community and approved by the Secretary of the Interior.
>
> (b) All children of at least one-fourth (1/4) degree Mdewakanton Sioux Indian blood born to an enrolled member of the Shakopee Mdewakanton Sioux Community.
>
> (c) All descendants of at least one-fourth (1/4) degree Mdewakanton Sioux Indian blood who can trace their Mdewakanton Sioux Indian blood to the Mdewakanton Sioux Indians who resided in Minnesota on May 20, 1886, Provided, they apply for membership and are found qualified by the governing body, and provided further, they are not enrolled as members of some other tribe or band of Indians.

The SMSC's official history confirms the tribe and its Constitution was federally recognized in 1969 with just thirteen adult charter members with voting privileges and twenty minors, and that Norman M. Crooks was the first chairman.

Norman M. Crooks, first chairman of the Shakopee Mdewakanton Sioux Community (SMSC).

For Leonard, reading the Constitution later was both inspiring and troubling. It clearly linked membership to the 1886 rolls and blood quantum, which gave it integrity. But it also carried a silence that worried him—the question of adoptions. "It was ambiguous and confusing," Leonard reflected. "No one argued about the 1886 rolls. No one argued about the quarter blood quantum. But the adoptions… that's where problems remain to this day."

Leonard also learned that the Bureau of Indian Affairs had repeatedly warned that removing the blood requirement by mere ordinance would "affect the very fabric of the Community" and could only be done by constitutional amendment.

Homeless Indians

The Constitution also drew directly from federal language that described Shakopee, Prairie Island, and Lower Sioux as lands reserved for "homeless Indians." This term, written into the 1886 agreements, had meant something precise: those Dakota left behind in Minnesota after 1862 who had been forced to sever ties with the exiled bands.

The Constitution underscored that point. No member of SMSC could belong to another tribe. To do so was to cancel one's status as a homeless Indian.

Leonard's mother saw in this an opportunity. Their father had declared membership at Lower Sioux, where he too was descended from the 1886 provisions. Under the rules, Leonard and his siblings, once they reached eighteen, would be entitled to apply at either Shakopee or Lower Sioux. His mother encouraged them to attend the meetings at which the Shakopee Constitution was being shaped. Leonard remembered the feeling vividly: "I slowly started to stick my big toe back into the world of my ancestors."

The Meetings

The early gatherings were held at Shakopee High School. Sometimes thirty attended, sometimes as many as forty-two. But the decisive meetings that finalized the Constitution were never widely announced. Many of those who had attended the earlier sessions were left out. Whether it was oversight or design, Leonard always believed Crooks had engineered the omission.

When the Constitution was ratified, only thirteen charter members appeared on the list. Unlike future applicants, they were not required to prove descent from the Henton or McLeod rolls. Their status was secure by fiat.

For the rest, the door had been closed.

Federal Oversight and Historical Burden

The Bureau of Indian Affairs supervised the constitutional process, drawing on the framework of the 1886 Congressional Act that had created three reservations: Lower Sioux, Prairie Island, and Shakopee. These lands had been a meager salvation for the "friendlies," those Dakota who had not joined the war.

At Lower Sioux the main camp had formed. Prairie Island was settled by others who did not wish to remain there. Shakopee's lands were unique; parcels purchased by Indian families—including Leonard's grandmother, Cecelia Campbell, who had bought eighty acres—that were later turned into trust lands.

For Leonard, the weight of history was inescapable. These families had faced impossible choices. With game disappearing and White settlers pressing in, survival itself was at stake. Some believed in fighting, others in farming, but those who abstained from the uprising became, in Congress's eyes, the "friendlies."

Their names were recorded in two censuses: the Henton Roll of 1863, listing full-blood Mdewakantons, and the McLeod Roll of 1886, which included both full-blood and mixed families. Together, about 220 individuals and their descendants became the legal core of Minnesota Dakota identity.

Tradition and Pragmatism

Even before 1862, Leonard understood, the Dakota had been divided. Some clung to traditional ways, rejecting assimilation. Others, more pragmatic, doubted victory was possible and turned to farming, reasoning that it was the only path to survival. Those who chose neutrality bore the mark of federal recognition. Their descendants were the ones for whom Shakopee, Prairie Island, and Lower Sioux were reserved.

The Constitution of 1969

The SMSC Constitution reflected that inheritance. It declared that the land would be held in trust for qualified applicants and provided for water, sewer, and housing improvements. Applicants had to show one-quarter blood descent from the 1886 rolls and residence in Shakopee.

Leonard would later write in a letter that the Constitution's language gave clarity on descent and blood quantum but left a dangerous gap. Adoption was not clearly addressed. Could the community vote to adopt those who did not meet the criteria? The silence created room for manipulation.

In the beginning, it seemed like a technical detail. In time, it would become the core of the enrollment wars. No one disputed the rolls. No one disputed the blood quantum. But adoptions would open the door to disputes that have raged across decades.

"The enrollment issue," Leonard reflected, "would become the bitter contest of our time. And it would feed the fury of a feud that never stopped—Crooks versus Prescott."

To Leonard, the rules were not obstacles but anchors. They tied his People to a specific history, one that mattered. The Rose Blossom crisis had shown him how easily they could be erased.

Leonard deeply understood the difference between being adopted into the tribe and being born from it. This distinction would shape not only his personal crusades but the larger wars of policy, governance, and memory. Adoptees—those without bloodline connection to the 1886 roll—were increasingly gaining access to

Tribal membership. Some were well-intentioned. Others, Leonard believed, were using legal mechanisms to claim rights they had not inherited, reshaping the community with political might and financial incentive.

At one point, the federal government itself had tried to help sort through the chaos. Mitchell Bush, head of enrollment for the Bureau of Indian Affairs, had worked with Leonard's administration to define who was qualified to hold land under the terms of the 1886 agreement. That agreement—rare and foundational—had long been the basis of the community's status. Without it, Tribal identity would become a matter of political whim.

A Compromise

Leonard's own daughter, Denise, had been caught in the storm. Though qualified by blood, she was forced to apply for membership as an adoptee, simply because the faction in power would not acknowledge her status. Leonard had resisted for two or three years, unwilling to let the adoption mechanism replace the rightful lineage. But Denise eventually came to him, saying, "I know your conviction, Dad, but I don't have anything. And if I could get adopted into the tribe, I would." And so, reluctantly, Leonard allowed it.

That decision—a father's compromise—haunted him. It encapsulated the heartache of a generation watching their community transform not through war or loss, but through quiet erosion. The constitutional rules, once sacred, were now pliable. Adoptees became voting members. They gained power, formed factions, rewrote the rules. And in Leonard's eyes, they rewrote the history.

"How can you have a constitution written by people who wouldn't have even been members under the rules they created?" he asked. "There are no adoptee Indians." This question wasn't rhetorical. It was the crux of a legal and spiritual battle for the soul of the community. The federal recognition granted in 1886 was not symbolic—it was legal. It conferred specific rights, defined Tribal landowners, and carried weight in the eyes of the United States government. Yet by the time Leonard told his story, more than 90 percent of those calling themselves members of the community were, in his estimation, not qualified under the original terms. That meant only 10 percent of the Shakopee Mdewakanton Sioux Community still carried the ancestral blood that had once defined its existence.

To Leonard, this was not just an identity crisis. It was Termination—quiet, bureaucratic, internal Termination. Not by federal decree. Not by military conquest. But by the community itself. And he carried that awareness like a wound.

A Letter of "Confession"

In 1975, under pressure to establish his eligibility to be a member of SMSC, the founder and charter member of the Mdewakanton community belatedly applied for membership.

In a brazen act of self-serving procedure, Norman M. Crooks signed a letter to SMSC on his own behalf declaring that he had been found eligible and his application for membership had been approved.

The signature on the letter shows the characteristic handwriting of his wife, Edith. Thus, the useless letter was not even signed by the chairman. The letter is an admission by Norm Crooks that he was not a member of SDMS at the time he founded the community and did not become a member until shortly before October 25, 1975.

SHAKOPEE MDEWAKANTON SIOUX COMMUNITY
OF
MINNESOTA
SHAKOPEE, MINNESOTA 55379

MARCH 26, 1975

NORMAN M. CROOKS Sr.
ROUTE 1 BOX 111
SHAKOPEE, MINN. 55379

Dear Member:

Your application for enrollment with the Shakopee Mdewakanton Sioux Community of Minnesota has been reviewed in accordance with the constitution and bylaws and the Act of October 25, 1972 (86 Stat. 1168). You have been determined to be eligible for membership and your name has been placed on the tribal roll.

Please advise the Aberdeen Area Office of any change in your mailing address. The Aberdeen Area Office is at 115 4th Ave. S.E., Aberdeen South Dakota 57401. Please mark your letter for the attention of Enrollment - Mississippi Sioux.

Sincerely yours,

Norman M Crooks
Chairman, Shakopee Mdewakanton
Sioux Community of Minnesota

This 1975 letter signed by Norman Crooks to himself declares that his application for membership in SDMS has been approved.

A Return to Spirit

By his mid-thirties, Leonard Prescott had carried the burdens of city life, family turmoil, and Tribal feuding. He had grown up between St. Paul's concrete and the fragile soil of the reservation, married a woman whose struggles with mental illness left him bewildered, and had watched as the politics of the Shakopee community hardened into rivalries and suspicion. He always thought of himself as Indian, but he knew deep down that his understanding of Dakota culture was fragmentary. He lacked the grounding that came from ceremony, story, and lived tradition.

It was during this restless period that Leonard experienced what he later called his *first spiritual awakening*. For years he had searched for answers about his direction in life. What would he do? Where did he belong? The answers came, unexpectedly, in ceremony.

His mother had long known Amos Owen and his wife, respected spiritual leaders at the Prairie Island Reservation near Red Wing, Minnesota. She had been acquainted with them since her teenage years and often spoke of Amos with reverence. He carried himself with quiet authority, conducting sweat lodges and guiding people who sought a way back into their culture. Eventually, she invited Leonard to come with her to Prairie Island to meet them.

For Leonard, that visit marked a turning point. At Prairie Island he felt for the first time the living presence of Dakota spirituality. He discovered a space where Indian People still spoke to the Grandfathers, to Wakȟáŋ Tȟáŋka, the Great Spirit, in the ways of old. In that circle, the ceremonies of the pipe and the sweat lodge opened to him, showing him a direction he had never known but had always needed.

The Gift of the Pipe

Among the first lessons Amos Owen shared was the story of the sacred pipe.

Long ago, Amos explained, two young hunters encountered a maiden in the forest among the stones. One was overwhelmed by unclean thoughts and attempted to approach her. At once he was reduced to dust. The other, filled with awe, recognized her as a spirit. He listened.

The maiden asked to be taken to the People. When the tribe gathered, she unwrapped a red cloth bundle and revealed what she carried: the pipe. It would be, she said, the means by which Indian People could speak to the Great Spirit for all time.

The teachings were precise. The stem of the pipe represented the human journey. Eagle feathers affixed to it signified the eagle, the messenger who could carry prayers upward. The most sacred element was tobacco. When placed in the pipe and burned, the smoke became the prayer itself. Drawn in and released, it rose skyward, borne by the eagle spirit to the Grandfathers.

The maiden told the People that from that day forward, the pipe would be their covenant with the Great Spirit. Then, as she walked away, she paused at the edge of the clearing. Turning back one final time, she transformed into a White Buffalo calf and disappeared into the forest.

For Leonard, this story became an anchor. The pipe was not a mere object; it was the embodiment of relationship. Every time tobacco was offered and smoke rose, the People were speaking to spirit in a line unbroken since that first gift.

The Lodge of Purification

Leonard's next teachings came in the sweat lodge. The sweat was about purification, sacrifice, and prayer. Its round shape represented the earth, while its interior symbolized the womb of Mother Earth. To enter it was to step back into creation itself, to be stripped down to spirit so that prayers could be carried cleanly to the heavens.

The fire was prepared with ritual care. Logs were stacked over rocks, and the rocks were heated until they glowed red. Fire keepers carried them to the lodge entrance. There the leader, using deer antlers to avoid the contamination of man-made materials, lifted each stone with prayer. Each was addressed as Grandfather, the oldest form of life, keeper of memory.

Participants entered the lodge counter-clockwise, following the natural order of the earth. The leader entered last. Inside, the Grandfather rocks were laid into the pit at the center—the womb of the earth—where cedar and sage were sprinkled upon them. Sage cleansed and purified; cedar burned away negative feelings.

The number of rocks varied according to the weight of the prayers. Twelve for a lighter round. Twenty-four, or even forty-two, for matters of great gravity. The more intense the need, the more stones, the greater the heat.

Songs greeted each Grandfather as it was welcomed inside. More songs rose with the prayers throughout the rounds. The darkness, steam, and heat enveloped everyone as their voices lifted together, their petitions borne upward through the cedar smoke.

Ceremony of the Pipe

At the conclusion of the sweat, the pipe returned. It was passed clockwise. Each participant received it, smoked, released prayers in smoke, then turned the pipe to the four directions—north, south, east, west—before pointing it downward to Mother Earth and upward to Father Sky.

Some prayed silently, their words hidden. Others prayed aloud so that the group might join their petitions. Each act was a thread woven into a collective prayer.

The spiritual leader, listening deeply, sometimes offered his interpretation of the messages carried upward. He would share impressions or words he believed had come from the Grandfathers, returning the answers to the People.

Leonard entered those lodges with longing. He was always searching for direction, unsure if the Grandfathers would speak, but hopeful. "It felt warm, safe," he said later. "It had a feeling of being in a spiritual presence, that something was going to happen."

It was in such a ceremony that Leonard received his Indian name. Bestowed by a spiritual leader, it was *Woyuonihan Kchi Nazin* — Stands With Honor.

The naming carried deep meaning. To be given a Dakota name was to be recognized by spirit, to be placed in relationship with community and tradition. For Leonard, it marked a shift in identity. After years of drifting, he now stood in a circle of belonging, bound by story, song, and prayer.

The Wider Movement

Leonard's awakening was not isolated. Across Indian Country in the 1970s, a wider resurgence of Native spirituality was underway. Termination policies had devastated communities, relocation had scattered families into cities, and boarding schools had silenced languages. Yet amidst this wreckage, ceremonies were being revived.

At Prairie Island, Amos Owen became a central figure. His sweat lodges were attended not only by Dakota but also by Ojibwe, Lakota, and even non-Native allies. His leadership was part of a broader spiritual revival that paralleled the political activism of the American Indian Movement. AIM gave voice to demands for sovereignty and treaty rights; spiritual leaders like Amos gave those demands a deeper foundation.

For Leonard, the convergence was powerful. AIM's protests had revealed the political urgency of survival. But in the sweat and with the pipe, he found the spiritual grounding that gave meaning to those struggles. Politics might fight for survival; spirituality gave it purpose.

Reflections on Leadership

In later years, as Leonard wrestled with the realities of Tribal governance, he often reflected on those first ceremonies at Prairie Island. The lessons of the pipe and the lodge shaped the way he thought about leadership.

He remembered how the pipe was passed clockwise, ensuring that every voice, however small, had a turn. He remembered how the sweat required entering counter-clockwise, in rhythm with the earth. The symbolism was clear—leadership was not about individual ambition, but about order, balance, and humility before something greater.

He contrasted this with the path of Norman Crooks, who had concentrated authority in himself, overriding the general council. Leonard could not forget Crooks' words: "Indians can't run these kinds of operations." That statement stood in sharp contrast to the teachings Leonard had received. The pipe had not been given to outsiders; it had been given to Indian People. The sweat was not led by contractors or management companies; it was led by Dakota elders.

"To me," Leonard reflected, "the lesson of the pipe was that sovereignty is ours to carry. No one else can carry it for us."

Standing with Honor

The teachings of Prairie Island did not erase Leonard's struggles. His community was still fractured. Feuds still tore at families. The work of building sovereignty and self-sufficiency lay ahead. But he was no longer lost. The pipe, the sweat, the songs, and the name he carried gave him a center.

He had become *Odaka Naghee*—Stands With Honor. From that center, he would confront the difficult choices of leadership, the battles over enrollment, and the challenges of building governance on sovereign ground.

In spirit, he had begun to stand with honor. In politics, he would soon have to prove it.

Bingo

Little Six: Origins of an Era

By the dawn of the 1980s, Indian Country was on the cusp of a transformation. Across the Nation, tribes were experimenting with high-stakes bingo as a means of exercising sovereignty and generating badly needed revenue. The Seminole Tribe of Florida had opened the first high-stakes operation in 1979, managed by the New England Entertainment Company. It proved wildly successful. Soon the same company partnered with the Cabazon Band of Mission Indians in California, again reaping extraordinary profits.

In their search for new opportunities, the management group turned its eyes northward. Their analysts noticed a small, barely resourced reservation thirty miles from downtown Minneapolis and thirty-five from St. Paul—the Shakopee Mdewakanton Sioux Community. On their own initiative, they conducted a market study of the Twin Cities region. With a median household income of $35,000–$42,000 and an estimated 15 percent in disposable income, the metro area looked like fertile ground for high-stakes bingo. With a potential market of nearly three million people, the opportunity gleamed.

The company identified the chairman of SMSC as Norman Crooks and made their approach. They wooed him with talk of Florida's success, with tours of Seminole facilities, with luxurious dinners and even a fishing trip. Crooks, impressed by both the spectacle and the figures, was convinced. Bingo, he told his People, could be the vehicle to carry Shakopee into prosperity.

A Proposal and a Constitution

But there was a hitch. Crooks first approached Marianna Schulstad, the field solicitor for the Bureau of Indian Affairs in Minneapolis. He asked if he, Norman Crooks, could start a high-stakes bingo hall on his personal lands. Schulstad was blunt. While tribes and Indian communities were sovereign, individuals were not. The hall could not be his personal venture. If he wanted the project, he would have to bring the proposal to the community.

Reluctantly, Crooks did so. In the spring of 1981, he presented the plan to SMSC members. The New England Entertainment Company would build a bingo hall, eventually named Little Six, for $1 million. In exchange, they would take 45 percent of the profits for fifteen years. SMSC would keep 55 percent but would receive no distributions until the building was paid off.

For an Indigenous People who had never managed a large-scale business, the offer seemed extraordinary. Millions in profit were predicted. Members voted in favor. They also resolved to divide their share: 45 percent for social programs, 55 percent for per capita distributions. For the first time, the dream of collective economic power seemed possible.

Building Little Six

Construction began in the spring of 1982, handled by New England Entertainment in partnership with Mulholwald Construction of

Prior Lake. The hall was modest by later standards—forty feet wide, a hundred feet long, fifteen feet high—but it could accommodate 1,200 customers. Its corrugated red metal shell covered insulation, and inside were rows of bolted-down tables, a small refreshment area, a raised podium for the bingo caller, and a back room for financial transactions.

Community members pitched in at the end—Leonard's siblings Pat and Alan, along with Crooks family members, Vigs, Rosses, Mattas, and others. They bolted chairs to the floor, positioned tables, and felt the growing excitement of a collective venture. For many, it was the first time they had touched the physical structure of their own economic future. Several of those who helped build Little Six would also become its first employees.

The hall was scheduled to open in early September. But persistent rains delayed construction and forced the building footprint to be shifted five feet north. Crooks presented this as an unavoidable necessity, but then used the shift to claim personal leverage.

Norm's Leverage

At a community meeting in late September 1982, Crooks delivered what he called "good news and bad news." The good news: Despite the rains, construction was complete. The bad news: The building now overlapped five feet of his personal property.

"What are you going to give me?" he asked the community.

The room fell silent. Darlene Matta spoke first, incredulous: "What do you mean, 'What are we going to give you?' What are you going to do if we don't give you anything?"

Crooks' reply stunned them: "I will bulldoze the building down."

Fear rippled through the members. The hall represented their hopes, their first real chance at collective success. Would he actually tear it down? No one could be sure. After tense discussion, Crooks proposed his price: 3 percent of the community's social service funds, payable to him for fifteen years. It would amount to about $2,000 a month for him, compared to roughly $300 per member in distributions.

Cornered, the community agreed. Leonard sat in the meeting, watching the dream of sovereignty bend under pressure. "We were standing on the brink of a huge success," he recalled. "And we were confronted with this roadblock. We felt we had no choice."

Opening Night

Despite the bitterness, anticipation grew. The New England Entertainment Company—soon to be renamed Pan American Gaming Enterprise—pushed toward opening. Their first manager, James Wilden, was forced out after suspected ties to organized crime. He was replaced by Fred Estrada, a Cuban-American with no such entanglements, who would remain in place throughout the relationship. A local insurance agent, Robert "Bob" Page, was hired to oversee daily transactions.

A marketing blitz promised a packed house for opening night. Of the 1,200 seats, half were reserved for Chicago junket players, half for Twin Cities residents. The plan backfired. On opening night, in October 1982, hundreds of Minnesotans were left outside, furious that seats had been given to out-of-staters.

Inside, the hall was jammed. Another hundred people were squeezed in, perching cards on countertops and even trash bin lids. The coverall prize was $80,000, and a brand-new Cadillac was raffled off. From the start, Little Six Bingo was a sensation. Nightly attendance averaged 800–850 players, with weekends sold out for years to come.

For five years, high-stakes bingo at Shakopee drew crowds, money, and the first glimmers of prosperity. But for Leonard Prescott, the triumph carried shadows: Crooks' personal deal, management's heavy hand, and the uneasy sense that sovereignty itself was being compromised.

The Little Six Bingo Palace open for business in late 1982.

Beginning of a Feud

Leonard's First Lessons as Treasurer

When Leonard Prescott entered Tribal leadership as treasurer, he was ushered into this new world. He was given a tour of the offices he would help oversee, working alongside Shirley Danz, the Tribal administrator. Danz handled day-to-day operations, money transactions from the hall, and served as Crooks' assistant in dealings with the Bureau of Indian Affairs. Leonard's role, at least on paper, seemed simple. He and the chairman co-signed every check that passed through SMSC's programs and its new gaming venture.

But Leonard quickly saw that gaming was not just about checks. It was about power, contracts, and the future of sovereignty itself.

Crooks, eager to demonstrate that bingo was a positive force for tribes, joined a national task force assembled by the BIA. In the fall of 1982, the Senate Select Committee on Indian Affairs convened hearings on the impact of bingo. Crooks, accompanied by SMSC's management company, Pan American Gaming, Inc., testified in Washington. They spoke of the hall's success and its contributions to social development. But Leonard noticed something troubling. Pan American's presence ensured that the interests of *management* were protected, sometimes more than the tribe's long-term goals of self-sufficiency, strong governance, and economic independence.

As Leonard later reflected, management companies in those early days "took advantage of unsuspecting Tribal groups." They knew that profits flowed not from their own brilliance, but from the legal and sovereign status of Tribal lands. Yet they negotiated contracts as though their own expertise was indispensable.

A Small Battle, A Larger Awakening

Into the spring of 1983, Leonard continued his weekly routine of check-signing at the administration office. At first it felt like little more than mechanical duty, but the repetition gave him a window into the community's financial life.

It was during this period that a day care worker named Merilee Welch approached him in distress. Merilee managed the tribe's new day care facility, a program for both residents and employees of the SMSC. She had just received her first performance evaluation from Administrator Shirley Danz, and she was devastated. The review, in her eyes, was dismissive of her efforts and minimized her contributions to a day care that had only been operating for six months. Tearfully, she asked Leonard to come downstairs and see her work for himself.

Leonard had never dealt with personnel matters before. His position as secretary–treasurer was financial, not administrative. But when he entered the day care, he saw order and care in every corner—tidy records, structured activities, a palpable sense of attention to the children. Merilee's management was methodical and full of heart. He left torn—sympathetic to her frustration, but uncertain whether he had any authority to intervene.

A few days later, Merilee pressed him again. Had anything changed? Had Shirley reconsidered? Leonard had expressed his concerns to the administrator, Shirley Danz, who had simply dismissed them and flatly stated the evaluation would stand. Merilee's insistence, however, stayed with him. Leonard had lived with enough pain of his own to recognize it in others, and he knew how much damage an unfair review could cause—not only to morale but to someone's future.

At the next business council meeting, Leonard raised the issue. Chairman Norm Crooks brushed it off immediately, saying he trusted his administrator. Vice Chairman Danny Crooks, Norm's son, stayed silent. The meeting moved on, leaving Leonard simmering.

After the meeting adjourned, Leonard followed Norm back into the conference room and pushed back on the issue. If anyone deserved a review, he told him, it was the administrator, Shirley Danz—certainly not Merilee. How could Shirley judge performance without ever setting foot in the day care and without witnessing Merilee's daily work? Leonard's rebuke was direct, sharper than he had ever delivered before.

Walking back down the stairs, he felt something stir—an unfamiliar pride. For the first time he sensed what it meant to stand up not merely as a signer of checks, but as a representative of employees and community alike. He had made a difference, however small, and Norm, though still guarded, seemed afterward to treat him with a new measure of respect. Or maybe concern.

Signs of Exclusion

In the months that followed, Leonard kept writing checks in Shirley Danz's office, stationed at a small table where he was half-ignored by managers and Pan American representatives who passed through on their way to the chairman. Slowly, they began addressing him by name, acknowledging that his presence could no longer be dismissed entirely.

That spring, the Bureau of Indian Affairs called on the community to participate in a broader project—distributing leftover accounting claims from the 1886 government settlements to qualified descendants in Minnesota, the Dakotas, and Nebraska. The SMSC would need to assemble genealogies and records, proving lineage back to the 1886 rolls in order to receive their share.

The business council traveled to Santee, Nebraska, for a Tribal meeting. Leonard rode in Norm's Ford van with Norm and Danny Crooks. What stayed with Leonard most was not the meeting itself, but a remark Norm made on the way: "You don't realize how good it feels not to have to work with those nit-picking women anymore."

It was a telling comment. The council was all-male now, and Leonard and Danny, both novices, had little more than symbolic roles. Norm controlled the conversations with the Bureau, projecting authority even though his own lineage to the 1886 rolls was unproven. With sheer confidence—and the support of those who wanted to believe—he had secured recognition as chairman.

Fairness in All Things

For Leonard, the irony was glaring. Members who could not produce a birth certificate or documented ties to the 1886 rolls were being brushed aside, while Norm Crooks, without solid proof of his own provenance, held court with federal officials. The imbalance gnawed at him.

The Merilee episode had awakened in him the conviction that fairness mattered—that a voice raised at the right time could protect someone overlooked. The trip to Santee deepened that conviction. If he could defend a day care worker against a skewed review, why could he not defend his entire community against skewed claims of leadership and legitimacy?

From that point forward, Leonard's role began to change. He was no longer content to be a passive observer at the check-signing table.

Slowly, almost reluctantly, he was stepping into the role of advocate. The struggle over enrollment, authenticity, and the meaning of the 1886 rolls would give him the cause he needed. And in defending that cause, he would begin to discover his own strength.

Crooks in Washington

Still, Norm Crooks' profile was growing, and he embraced it. In 1982, the Bureau of Indian Affairs invited him to join a national task force studying the impact of bingo on trust lands. That fall, the Senate Select Committee on Indian Affairs convened hearings. Crooks traveled to Washington, accompanied by representatives of Pan American. Together, they testified to bingo's benefits: jobs created, programs funded, communities lifted.

For Leonard, this testimony was telling. It presented bingo as a triumph, but it also underscored management's dominance. Pan American's polished voices emphasized stability and growth. Less was said about sovereignty, about building internal capacity, about learning to manage enterprises without dependence. "They were protecting their interests," Leonard later observed, "not necessarily ours."

Paid-Off Hall, New Promises

Despite these concerns, bingo was a windfall. By May 1983, Crooks proudly announced at a special meeting that the bingo hall had been paid off in full. Members erupted in applause. For the first time, there was surplus. The general council approved per capita distributions of $300, while also resolving to fund the following community needs:

- a day care center so parents could work without fear for their children
- a dental office to provide local care
- an expanded accounting office to handle the swelling revenues

For Leonard, these moments captured the promise of sovereignty. For the first time in living memory, SMSC was building its own infrastructure.

The Cultural Center Dream

Flush with success, Crooks unveiled an even grander vision: a cultural center that would house Dakota artifacts and tell the story of survival. Crowned with an 85-foot teepee, the building would cover 2,000 square feet. Crooks boasted that he had already purchased nearly a quarter of a million dollars' worth of artifacts from Ario Hause, a self-styled "adopted member" of the tribe.

Pan American agreed to finance the project for $350,000. Construction moved forward. But when the building was three-quarters complete, the company returned with bad news: Costs had soared to $550,000, and funds were exhausted.

Their proposed solution was unsettling. Until the debt was covered, the building could be used for experimental games—table games modeled on blackjack and craps but legally disguised with bingo mechanics. These games had already been rejected in Florida. Pan American suggested SMSC try them anyway. Revenues would pay off the shortfall, after which the building could be rededicated as a cultural center.

A Handshake, Not a Vote

Crooks rejected Leonard's proposal to renegotiate with Pan American. In a general council meeting, he defended his decision bluntly in these tribe-deprecating words: "Indians can't run these kinds of operations. We need the management company to continue operations." He announced that he had already signed a contract with Pan American extending the 55/45 split and the fifteen-year term.

Then, in a gesture that would haunt the community, Crooks clasped hands with Fred Estrada of Pan American and declared, "Fred Estrada is an honorable man, and I am a man of my word. It's done."

The general council, which was the community's highest governing body, had not been consulted on this important agreement. SMSC's Constitution stated clearly that the chairman could act only at the direction of the general council. The business council was to carry out those directives, not override them. Crooks' decision clearly violated the Constitution outright.

The general council was stunned. SMSC's Constitution was explicit—the chairman could act only on the direction of the council. The business council was to implement, not override, its decisions. Crooks had broken that covenant.

Fallout

When the meeting ended, members clustered outside, angry and bewildered. Many felt as though their constitutional rights had been stolen. Families gathered at Leonard's mother's house to discuss strategy. Around her kitchen table, they spoke of betrayal, of arrogance, of the need to defend the general council's authority.

They sent Leonard back to Crooks, hoping he might reconsider. Crooks entertained the conversation but offered no real concession. The construction continued, and so did management's control.

For Leonard, this was the turning point. The sweat lodges at Prairie Island had taught him that every voice mattered, that sovereignty rested in the circle. What he saw now was one man signing away the will of his People with a handshake.

The rift was deepening. The Crooks–Prescott feud had begun.

The Fall of a Chairman

By 1984, the Shakopee Mdewakanton Sioux Community had reached a breaking point. The general council's authority had been undermined repeatedly by Chairman Norman Crooks, who continued to act unilaterally in defiance of the Constitution. His handshake deals with Pan American Gaming had locked the tribe into lopsided contracts. His claim that "Indians can't run these kinds of operations" was now seared in memory as an insult to sovereignty itself.

For Leonard Prescott and others, the question had shifted from policy to survival. Could the community continue under a chairman who disregarded the very document that defined their existence as a self-governing people?

The Fight for Removal

The first move was procedural. After Crooks had flatly refused to renegotiate with Pan American, members of the general council began to gather again in private homes. Most often it was at the house of Leonard's mother, Rose Blossom, where she, his sister Pat, Allene Ross, and Susan Togenhagen pored over the Constitution. They knew its provisions well, and they reminded Leonard that one clause allowed for the removal of officers who had gone too far. The process was demanding: One-third of the membership had to sign a petition, which the vice chairman was then required to serve on the chairman.

The petition was circulated, signatures collected. By the Constitution's measure, it was valid. But the vice chairman was Danny Crooks—Norm's son. Members were uneasy asking Danny to deliver removal papers to his father, so they pressed Leonard, as secretary□treasurer, to approach him. Leonard did so, and Danny refused. His refusal was more than personal—it was itself a violation of constitutional duty. The process ground to a halt.

The group returned to Leonard's mother's kitchen, frustrated but determined. They decided to seek outside advice. Leonard's mother suggested Larry Leventhal, a Minneapolis attorney well-known for defending the American Indian Movement during the Wounded Knee trials, a man steeped in both courtroom craft and Native law.

Leventhal welcomed them into his office, listened carefully, and read through their Constitution. His advice was clear: change the ordinance. Draft a petition to allow the secretary–treasurer to serve removal papers if the vice chair refused, and, if necessary, allow any general council member to serve them if both officers failed. Armed with this strategy, the group presented a new petition. Norm, bound by the rules he had so often bent, was forced to call a meeting.

A Meeting in Chaos

The meeting was held within ten days. Norm, Danny, and Leonard arrived first. Norm and his son were cold, their hostility thinly veiled.

When a quorum gathered, members voiced their anger—not only at the constitutional evasions but at the very idea that their chairman could sign contracts and cut deals without their consent.

Norm grew heated, his patience snapping. "I no longer want to be in this meeting," he shouted. "I'm leaving." Danny followed him out.

The general council was stunned. The chairman had abandoned the chair. The vice chairman had abandoned his duty. For a moment, it seemed the Constitution itself had been rendered useless. Leonard turned to Leventhal, who had come to the meeting. "What can we do?" he asked.

Put on the spot, Leventhal steadied himself. Under Robert's Rules of Order, he explained, if the presiding officer refused to lead, the assembly had the right to appoint its own. A motion was made and seconded. Leonard, as secretary–treasurer, was appointed pro tempore chairman for the meeting. Under his gavel, the council voted to amend the ordinance. For the first time, they had maneuvered around Norm's intransigence with constitutional precision.

Cold Nights and False Starts

With the ordinance amended, a new petition circulated. Leonard was now authorized to serve removal papers himself. In September 1984, he set out on a cold, rainy night to Norm's home. His cousin Michael answered the door, nervous and unsure. When Leonard explained his purpose, Michael hesitated: "My dad's not going to be very happy with this."

Norm appeared behind him, face red with fury. He lunged at the doorway, smashing his shoulder against the frame. Leonard dropped the petition inside and walked back to his van. The deed was done.

Or so they thought.

When the council met, Norm did not appear. The petition, the Bureau of Indian Affairs later ruled, had been served outside the required time frame. The entire effort was invalid.

The Third Attempt

The group did not quit. They combed through membership rolls, identifying supporters, fence-sitters, and opponents. Leonard himself went door-to-door, explaining the need for removal, making the case one household at a time. This was more than a petition drive—it was a civic education in sovereignty.

The third petition gained signatures from more than half the general council, far surpassing the one-third requirement. This time, Leonard served his uncle Norman Crooks at the Tribal office. Norm reluctantly accepted the papers without outburst.

The council met. The vote was taken. The removal of Norman Crooks as chairman was complete. Norm walked out immediately. His son Danny, who had succeeded him by order of succession, stood long enough to protest: "If this is the way you're going to treat my father, I don't want anything to do with this community. I resign."

Outside the community building, the press was waiting—the *Minneapolis StarTribune*, the *Saint Paul Pioneer Press*, and TV stations WCCO, KARE11 and KMSP. Reporters crowded Danny as he tried to reach his truck, shouting questions: "What are you guilty of?" Cameras flashed. He slammed the door shut and sped away.

For the Crooks family, it was devastation. Never before had the community seen such a spectacle. For the general council, it was a turning point. The Constitution, for all its fragility, had teeth. For the first time, the council had asserted its authority and won.

With Norm removed and Danny resigned, only one officer remained. At thirty-four years old, Leonard Prescott was now acting chairman of the Shakopee Mdewakanton Sioux Community. It was not a role he had sought. But sovereignty rarely waits for readiness.

The Shadow of Pan American

Norm's removal did not end the crisis. In his absence, the tribe still faced a management company entrenched in operations and unwilling to relinquish control. Pan American Gaming, once courted as savior, now appeared as overlord. Their contracts were still in force, their personnel still in the building, their grip on cash and authority intact.

For Leonard, stepping into the role of acting chairman, the challenge was stark. The tribe had reclaimed its Constitution, but not yet its economy.

The confrontation came at the Little Six Bingo Hall. Leonard and a group of members entered the building with the knowledge that sovereignty demanded more than words—it required possession. Pan American managers tried to block the way, insisting that operations were theirs to control. Leonard, backed by community members, pushed past them.

It was not an orderly transition. Voices rose, accusations flew, and the tension was electric. But in the end, Leonard and his supporters asserted their right. Pan American was finished. The tribe would run its own hall.

Desperation

When Pan American finally lost its grip, the Shakopee community inherited not a turnkey business but a circus of half-locked doors, chained entrances, and an empty money room. The irony was heavy. After years of being told by Chairman Crooks and his management allies that "Indians can't run these kinds of operations," the community now found itself running the show—without keys, without cash, and with little more than determination.

The transition was hardly elegant. On the eve of reopening, Leonard, his sister Pat, and a handful of others—seven or eight in all—literally blocked the door to keep Pan American out. When Fred Estrada, Pan American's representative, threatened federal court action, Leonard hung up on him and called his cousin Jeannie. By the time they reached the hall, Pan American's security guards had already chained the back door. Leonard climbed a hill, slipped in another way, and shoved past guards as they were closing up. "You can't keep me out of this building," he told them. "I'm a member of this community. I'm an officer of the community."

The guards urged reason. Leonard replied that reason had already run its course. The contract was invalid. "This is our building. If Pan American won't run the hall, we will."

The guards left. The tribe walked in. Sovereignty, reclaimed, began with an occupation.

Pat Prescott, until then the assistant manager, was suddenly promoted by circumstance to general manager of Little Six Bingo. But the new management team quickly discovered they had none of the basics—no keys to the money room, no operating cash, not even access to chips.

The solution was as improvised as it was symbolic. Leonard and others climbed through ceiling tiles, dropped down into the money room, and rummaged for whatever could be salvaged. They found chips—but no money. The management company had cleaned out the safe.

Pat calculated what they would need to reopen the next night—$1,500 in cash.

A Humble Loan

Leonard went looking. He first approached the VFW, to which he had donated a $20,000 van. He asked for a $1,500 loan from the bartender, but he had no authority. Then, on a whim, he drove to the Red Owl grocery store in Prior Lake, hoping to find Cleve, the store's owner. Cleve wasn't there. His manager, skeptical, told Leonard, "Cleve doesn't lend anybody money."

But Leonard persisted. He explained that the community had lost its management company and was scrambling to keep Little Six open. The manager dialed Cleve at home. Over the phone, Leonard made his case. To his surprise, Cleve agreed. "You're a businessman, I'm a businessman," he said. "I know who you are. I'll back you."

Cleve instructed his manager to take money from every till in the store—cash from each register, gathered after hours. Leonard walked out with $1,500 in grocery money stuffed into his pockets. When he returned, Pat was astonished. She hadn't believed he would get it.

Then she recalculated their needs. "Actually, we'll need $2,000."

That extra $500 felt like a mountain. There was no one else to ask. By morning, even worse news arrived. The safe couldn't be opened, locked on a time release. When it was finally opened, it held no cash at all. Pan American had taken everything.

For a moment, it looked as if the tribe's first independent attempt at gaming might collapse before it began.

Then the phone rang. It was Brinks Security, the armored-car company that had long transported cash from Little Six. The dispatcher had seen a newspaper story about the turmoil at Shakopee and asked, "We have a load of money from the bingo hall. Who do we deliver it to?"

Leonard didn't hesitate. "Bring it here."

Soon, a Brinks truck rolled up, delivering $10,000 in cash to the money room. Against all odds, the lights would stay on.

When Pan American learned that Leonard had intercepted the Brinks delivery of $10,000, they called the police claiming that an officer of SMSC had stolen the money that Pan American was responsible for. In the end, it became clear that the tribe could not steal money from itself, and the money had never belonged to Pan American. The result was growing bitterness between the parties.

Ironies of Sovereignty

Thus began the community's first week as its own manager—climbing through ceilings for chips, borrowing grocery store cash after hours, and accepting a lifeline from Brinks. What had been predicted as impossible—Indians running their own operation—was underway, albeit with comic fits and desperate improvisations.

In hindsight, Leonard could see the irony clearly. Sovereignty did not arrive with polished ledgers or professional suits. It arrived with borrowed cash in paper bags, ceiling tiles left askew, and the faint smell of Red Owl groceries on the tribe's first bankroll.

It was, by every measure, a meager beginning. But it was theirs.

Picking Up the Pieces

With Pan American gone and Crooks out of office, the Shakopee Mdewakanton Sioux Community faced the daunting work of rebuilding. The books were a mess, the staff inexperienced, and faith in leadership badly shaken. Every dollar mattered. Every night's game at Little Six was a test of survival.

Leonard and the business council had to move quickly. Cash flow systems were reorganized. Reliable employees were hired and trained. Accounting processes, long left in the hands of outside managers, were slowly wrested back under Tribal control. Mistakes were inevitable, but each correction marked progress.

For many members, it was the first time they saw their tribe not simply as a community but as an enterprise—something that had to be managed, sustained, and defended.

The community itself was divided in mood. Some felt relief that Crooks was gone, believing his arrogance and unilateral deals had nearly sunk their future. Others mourned the rupture, uneasy with the public spectacle of removal and the bitter wounds it left in families. The Crooks name, once synonymous with leadership, now evoked betrayal for some and loyalty for others.

But amid the divisions, there was a fragile pride. Members knew they had stood up for their Constitution, reclaimed their hall, and proven that sovereignty meant something more than words on paper. They had risked everything to take back what was theirs, and they had won—if only barely.

For Leonard, the burden was heavy. At thirty-four, he had become acting chairman in the most volatile circumstances imaginable. He bore the anger of those still loyal to Crooks, the expectations of those who wanted immediate results, and the practical nightmare of stabilizing a multimillion-dollar operation with almost no preparation.

He carried those pressures quietly, leaning on the discipline he had built over years of struggle. Nights in the sweat lodge and lessons with the pipe had taught him that sovereignty was not abstract—it was lived in the choices of each day, each meeting, each risk taken for the survival of the People.

Lessons of the Crisis

The various crises left enduring lessons. It revealed how vulnerable a community could be to outside manipulation when it lacked internal expertise. It showed how fragile sovereignty was when one man, however charismatic, could sign away the will of the people. And it underscored that reclaiming control was never tidy—it came through confrontation, confusion, and the scramble for survival.

Most of all, it proved that the general council mattered. Its voice, once disregarded, had forced change. Its determination had pushed past intimidation and bulldozer threats. In that moment, the People themselves had acted as the true custodians of sovereignty.

The removal of Norm Crooks and the expulsion of Pan American marked the end of one chapter and the beginning of another. SMSC was no longer a passive recipient of contracts and percentages. It was now an owner, a manager, a sovereign Nation responsible for its own enterprise.

The path ahead would not be smooth. New challenges loomed—membership disputes, political rivalries, the question of how to grow beyond bingo. But the lesson of those chaotic months was seared into memory. Never again would the community surrender its future with a handshake.

For Leonard Prescott, the young acting chairman who had stood at the center of it all, the experience was transformative. The boy who had once wandered the streets of St. Paul searching for direction was now a leader entrusted with the survival of his People.

And though the weight was immense, he carried it—because sovereignty demanded nothing less.

Entangling Enrollment and Gaming

The battles over contracts and percentages were never just about money. Beneath them lay a deeper question—who legally belonged to the community?

The 1969 Constitution had been clear on certain points. Membership rested on descent from the 1886 rolls—the McLeod and Henton lists of "loyal Mdewakanton" families who had not joined the uprising of 1862. Applicants had to prove at least one-quarter blood and residence at Shakopee. Yet the Constitution had been ambiguous on the matter of adoptions—whether individuals without full qualifications could be brought into the tribe by vote or ordinance.

That ambiguity, at first a footnote, became a fault line once gaming money began to flow. Sovereignty, once an abstract principle, was now measured in monthly distributions, in the power to decide who received $300 checks and who did not. With Little Six packed night after night and profits climbing, the question of enrollment grew sharper.

Norm Crooks had understood this terrain. By controlling contracts with management companies and extending deals without council approval, he had already demonstrated his willingness to act decisively. He also knew that expanding the rolls through adoption would build him a loyal base, cementing his power in general council meetings.

Leonard saw this as a betrayal of the Constitution's intent. The rolls of 1886 were not an arbitrary list; they were the federal recognition of those Dakota families who had chosen survival in Minnesota after 1862, severing ties to the exiled bands. To dilute that inheritance through adoptions was, in his view, to undermine the very legitimacy of the community.

The connection between gaming contracts and enrollment battles was thus forged. Revenues made membership valuable; membership disputes made revenues a weapon.

Kitchen Table Politics

In those years, the Prescott house became a hub of resistance. After council meetings, families would gather in Leonard's mother's kitchen to voice frustrations. Some spoke of the unfairness of Crooks' personal deal—the 3 percent cut for the five feet of land. Others worried about the fifteen-year contract he had signed without approval. Still others focused on enrollment, on the growing list of names being added without clear proof of descent.

For Leonard, the conversations all linked back to a single principle—*sovereignty must rest with the People.* The Constitution had enshrined that authority in the general council. Crooks' actions—

signing contracts alone, approving adoptions without consensus—stripped that sovereignty away.

Leonard often contrasted these political struggles with the teachings he had received at Prairie Island. In the sweat lodge, each person entered in turn, counter-clockwise, honoring the natural order. Each voice was heard. Each prayer was carried upward. Authority came from the circle, not the individual.

Now, in Shakopee, he watched as one man bypassed the circle, declaring himself the sole voice of the People. The dissonance was stark.

The Feud Deepens

By the mid-1980s, the lines were clear. Crooks represented consolidation—contracts signed, adoptions approved, management defended. Prescott represented resistance—the insistence on constitutional process, on fidelity to the 1886 rolls, on renegotiating for stronger terms.

What had begun as a debate over percentages and contracts now had become a community-defining feud. Families aligned on either side. Old grievances resurfaced. Every meeting carried the possibility of confrontation.

Leonard knew the struggle was larger than personal rivalry. It was about whether sovereignty meant self-determination for the People or convenience for a single chairman and his partners.

A Turning Point

The early years of Little Six had brought undeniable prosperity. The hall was packed, the debt retired, distributions begun, new programs funded. But beneath the applause lay a growing unease. The very success of gaming had exposed the community's weaknesses: its inexperience in business, its vulnerability to outside management, its divisions over membership.

For Leonard, the realization was sobering. Sovereignty was not self-executing. It required vigilance, unity, and fidelity to principle. Without those, it could be bartered away with a handshake.

The Crooks–Prescott feud would rage for years, but its roots lay in the corrugated red walls of Little Six, in the applause of opening night, in the whispered anger outside council meetings, and in the prayers Leonard carried from the sweat lodge into the storm of Tribal politics.

PART 3:
Chairman Leonard Prescott

The Aftermath

The removal of Norm Crooks had been decisive, but it did not bring calm. If anything, the weeks that followed felt more turbulent. The Pan American contract had been shattered, the management company forced from the reservation, and the SMSC suddenly found itself holding the keys to its own bingo hall. Sovereignty had been reclaimed on paper—but in practice it was chaos.

Leonard now had both a platform and a storm. He stood at the head of a community scarred by betrayal, fractured by suspicion, and inexperienced in governance. The weight of expectation was immense—to prove that Shakopee could govern itself, to show that its sovereignty was not just symbolic but practical.

The Pan American crisis had taught him that sovereignty was more than a word. It was a daily discipline, messy and demanding, requiring courage, patience, and constant vigilance. And now, with the chairman's gavel in his hand, Leonard Prescott resolved to try.

The shadow of Pan American lingered long after their departure. The contract had been broken, their managers dismissed, their handshakes exposed as false—but the residue of mistrust was everywhere. It seeped into family conversations, into council meetings, into the very air of the bingo hall.

Leonard carried the memories of those desperate nights like scars. He remembered climbing into ceiling tiles with a flashlight, searching for hidden stashes of cash that Pan American might have tucked away. He remembered the hollow feeling of coming up empty, the knowledge that without money for payouts, the hall might collapse on the spot.

He recalled how a local grocer first came to the rescue with an emergency loan so the tribe could limp through the night's games. Then, as the fear deepened, the sight of a Brinks truck pulling onto the reservation with $10,000 in operating cash felt almost biblical—a modern-day manna that allowed the community to survive another day.

Those humiliations were burned into Leonard's mind. They revealed how thin sovereignty could feel when it was backed by no reserves, no cushion, no expertise. Independence, in those moments, looked less like triumph and more like survival.

The parking lot became another battlefield. Arguments over contracts, payouts, and council decisions spilled outside, sometimes into fists. Patrons walked past, clutching their bingo cards, while community members shouted at one another under the glow of the streetlights. The very space meant to represent progress had become a theater of division.

Leonard understood the symbolism. For generations, White men had used contracts and promises to divide Dakota People against themselves. Now, even without the outsiders present, those old suspicions still poisoned the well. Every deal, every check, every whispered rumor carried the question: *Are we once again being cheated? Are we even capable of governing ourselves?*

A Reluctant Chair

Leonard never intended to hold the office. In his mind, once Pan American was gone and stability returned, he would step aside, return to Naegele Outdoor Advertising or the sheet metal trade, and leave leadership to others.

During the petition drive, Susan Totenhagen of the Brewer family had already voiced her ambition. She wanted the chairmanship, and at that time, Leonard, who was still thinking of himself as a temporary steward, promised to support her.

But when the dust settled, when Norm was removed and the council needed a new leader, the members turned to Leonard. The same people who had trusted him to push out Pan American insisted that he stay. They were not convinced Susan could lead. They wanted the man who had proven himself in the fight.

It was not the outcome Leonard expected, nor the one he desired. But it was the outcome the people demanded.

Susan came straight to his house when she heard he had won the chair. Leonard recalled the sting of her words at the door: "I thought you wanted to resign. I thought you were going to step aside."

He tried explaining that the members had asked him. They felt secure with him. They needed him to stay. But after these feeble attempts to clarify, Susan's face crumpled with disbelief, then hardened with sorrow. She turned away without another word.

Leonard watched her leave, knowing he had lost a friend and gained an opponent. The chairmanship had not yet begun, and already the battle lines were forming.

The Burden of Conviction

Leonard carried that weight heavily. He was thirty-four, untested, and suddenly responsible for the governance of a fractured community. His own conviction was simple—leadership had to be about trust and fairness. It could not be about family gain or personal power.

"To me," Leonard reflected, "leadership is not for the betterment of oneself or one's family, but for the betterment of the society it is charged to lead." He framed his agenda in two layers. The *difficult but possible* layer was economic growth, rooted in bingo and expanding to other ventures. The *impossible dream* layer was rational, transparent Tribal governance—something that had eluded not just Shakopee but Native communities across the country in the early years of newfound economic promise.

Even as chairman, Leonard could not escape the memory of those desperate nights that preceded his elevation to chairman. Every decision he and the council made was colored by the community's fear of mismanagement, by the scars of a contract that had siphoned profits away from the community. When fights broke out in the parking lot, when families whispered suspicions about where the money was going, Leonard felt the echoes of Pan American's manipulations. The tribe had learned, painfully, that sovereignty could be squandered if vigilance faltered.

The mistrust that had been sown by outside contracts did not vanish with their removal. Mistrust lingered, poisoning relationships inside the community. Leonard understood too well that the greatest threat was no longer Pan American, but Shakopee's own internal divisions.

A New Council

To steady the ship, Leonard moved quickly. He offered Susan the vice-chair position, honoring in part the promise he had once made. She accepted reluctantly, her disappointment still fresh. For secretary–treasurer, Leonard put forward his cousin Allene Ross, respected for her youth work and her skill with numbers. Together, they formed a slate, and together they were elected.

For the first time, Leonard felt he had a council that reflected the broader will of the people, not just one family's power. The Crooks family, realizing their numbers had slipped, grew quieter.

The council's first priority was obvious—tighten oversight of the bingo hall. For months, they still worked with Pan American, which hinted at renegotiation, but Leonard had no illusions. Outside managers could not be trusted to value Tribal assets properly.

From Firefighting to Framework

Leonard knew he could not spend his tenure forever patching holes and scrambling for cash. The Brinks truck had saved them once, but salvation by emergency delivery was no way to run a Nation. If the community was to survive—not just financially but spiritually—it needed more than luck. It needed structure.

The first step was *oversight*. Leonard insisted that every financial transaction, every payroll, and every expense be reviewed not only by the administrator but also by the business council. It was an exhausting process, requiring long evenings with ledgers and receipts, but after the dark days of ceiling tiles and missing cash, there could be no shortcuts.

He also pressed for *training Tribal members* to step into management roles. For years, the community had been told they were incapable of running their own affairs—that outsiders were necessary to handle contracts, finances and operations. Pan American had leaned on that prejudice like a crutch, repeating it until even some members began to believe it. Leonard rejected the idea. Sovereignty, he said, was not just a legal shield but a skill that had to be practiced. If his People were ever to be free of outside managers, they had to learn how to manage themselves.

The work was slow, frustrating, and full of setbacks. Mistakes were made. Employees trained on the job often stumbled through the unfamiliar responsibilities of cash flow and scheduling. Council meetings dragged late into the night, bogged down in arguments about who should hold which responsibility. And always, in the background, the factions whispered. Some accused Leonard of moving too cautiously, others of being reckless.

Still, progress came in small but steady steps. Accounting systems grew clearer. Job descriptions became standardized. Council records, once scattershot, were formalized. These were not glamorous reforms, but they were essential.

A Fragile Authority

The irony was not lost on Leonard. He had become chairman not because of ambition, but because of necessity. His authority remained fragile, contested not only by his opponents but also by the very history of his People. Centuries of broken promises had left them skeptical of any leader, even one of their own.

In quiet moments, Leonard would recall the lessons of the sweat lodge—the hot stones welcomed as Grandfathers, the smoke rising with prayers. In those ceremonies he had learned that purification came not all at once, but in waves, with endurance and patience. Governing the SMSC felt much the same. Each meeting was a round of heat and sweat, each reform a prayer that the community might find its footing.

For the first time, Leonard began to glimpse what a path forward might look like. It would not be swift, and it would not be without opposition. But it would be theirs.

A Wider Lens

Leonard knew Shakopee's battles were not unique. Across Indian Country, numerous Tribal governments were wrestling with the same questions: How do you protect sovereignty when every deal with outsiders seems to chip away at it? How do you run a modern business when your People have been deliberately denied the tools of governance for generations? How do you build unity in a community fractured by poverty, jealousy, and centuries of mistrust?

The rise of Tribal gaming in the late 1970s and early 1980s had sharpened those dilemmas. The Seminoles of Florida had been first, opening high-stakes bingo in 1979 with the backing of the very management company that later came knocking in Shakopee. Their success was explosive, but so too were the controversies. The state fought to regulate them, investors swooped in with contracts tilted to their advantage, and community members often found themselves excluded from the very profits their sovereignty had made possible.

The Cabazon Band in California fought a similar battle, opening their own gaming enterprise only to face lawsuits and harassment from state authorities. By the mid-1980s, the question of Indian gaming had reached the federal courts and would soon reach Congress itself. Shakopee was hardly alone in its turbulence. It was part of a national storm.

In that storm, Leonard's conviction only deepened. He believed that the SMSC's survival depended on learning from the mistakes of others. Contracts could not be signed lightly. Outside managers could not be trusted to value Tribal assets fairly. And most of all, governance had to be built from within, however slowly, however painfully.

He sometimes thought of his own journey—from the boy selling newspapers in the Snake Pit, to the young man caught between gangs on Saint Paul's West Side, to the thirty-four-year-old suddenly thrust into the chairmanship of a sovereign Nation. His life had been shaped by lessons of toughness, survival, and fairness. Now, those same lessons had to be applied at the level of a community.

Echoes of History

The work reminded Leonard constantly of older patterns. For centuries, the Dakota had been told they could not manage their own lands, their own treaties, their own affairs. The removal, the broken promises, the land seizures—all had been justified by the same logic—*Indians can't manage themselves.*

Now, in the age of bingo and high-stakes gaming, the language was the same. When Norm Crooks defended the Pan American contract, he said, "Indians can't run these kinds of operations. We need the management company." Those words rang in Leonard's ears as both an insult and a challenge.

He was determined to prove the opposite.

A Lonely Conviction

But determination did not erase loneliness. Leonard often found himself isolated between factions—criticized by those who thought he leaned too heavily on reform, doubted by those who feared he was too soft on outside partners. Every decision was contested, every reform second-guessed.

He thought back to the day care worker, Merilee Welch, and her tearful plea for fairness. Standing up for her, even though he was not successful, had been Leonard's first real step into leadership. Now, as chairman, he saw the same struggle magnified across the entire community. Fairness was not just a principle. It was a practice, and practicing it meant standing in the fire of other people's anger.

Yet, for Leonard, there was no turning back. Sovereignty had to be defended, not in lofty speeches, but in ledgers, contracts, and the daily grind of governance. It was slow, unglamorous work—but it was the only path forward.

Vision Beyond Bingo

The bingo hall had saved the community, but Leonard knew it could not be the end of the story. High-stakes games might keep the lights on and fill the per capita envelopes, but a People could not live on payouts alone. Sovereignty meant more than survival—it meant the ability to chart a future.

From the first days of his chairmanship, Leonard began to think in longer terms. What industries could be built beyond gaming? What services could be created to make the community self-sufficient rather than dependent on contracts and outside managers? What cultural spaces could anchor the People not only in prosperity but in memory?

He was not naïve about the difficulties. Every suggestion was met with suspicion. Proposals for new projects ignited old fears—*Who will profit? Who will control? Will it divide us further?* Yet Leonard pressed forward, believing that planning for the future was the surest way to honor the past.

His vision carried two parts. The first was economic—to expand beyond bingo into diversified enterprises that would generate steady revenue—construction, hospitality, and eventually other forms of gaming as the national legal landscape shifted. The second was cultural—to create places where Dakota history and spirituality could be taught, remembered and lived. A cultural center, a day care, a dental clinic—these were not just programs, they were declarations that Shakopee could care for its own.

Against the Grain

The irony, of course, was that Leonard's vision demanded resources that barely existed. In the wake of Pan American's departure, cash was tight, expertise thin, and trust thinner still. Every step toward diversification looked, to some, like overreach. Why not just let the bingo hall run and enjoy the per capita checks? Why risk it all on dreams?

But Leonard had seen enough of dependency to know it was a dead end. He thought of his mother, Rose Blossom, shuttling between communities and struggling with the tangled rules of enrollment. He thought of his father's disconnection from Shakopee. He thought of the countless times Native People had been told to wait, to settle, to make do. He would not let Shakopee settle.

Just as important as the money was the culture. Leonard's own path back to Dakota spirituality had been slow and uncertain. The sweat lodges of Amos Owen, the teachings of the pipe, the stories of the White Buffalo calf woman—these had given him a sense of grounding, a reminder that sovereignty was spiritual before it was financial.

If Shakopee was to prosper, it had to reconnect to those roots. Economic growth without cultural revival would hollow out the People, leaving them wealthy but lost. In every council meeting, Leonard carried that conviction quietly, even if it was not always understood.

A Narrow Path

The headwinds remained strong. Factions continued to feud. Old rivalries lingered. The legacy of mismanagement had left scars that would take years to heal. Yet Leonard understood that leadership was not about the easy path but about the necessary one.

He would often recall the phrase he had adopted early in his tenure: *The difficult we'll do right now; the impossible will take a little while.* Bingo was the difficult. True governance, true sovereignty, true cultural renewal—that was the impossible.

But for Leonard, impossible did not mean hopeless. It meant worthy.

Dreams are easy to speak and hard to build. Within months of becoming chairman, Leonard found himself testing the boundaries of what the community would allow. The idea of diversification—venturing into projects beyond bingo—was greeted with raised eyebrows. Some members saw it as ambition beyond their reach. Others suspected it as a cover for favoritism. And still others, weary from decades of disappointment, simply wanted the comfort of per capita checks and nothing more.

Leonard pressed anyway. He reminded the general council that bingo had not been guaranteed either. It had been born in controversy, nearly strangled by bad contracts, and held together by sheer determination. If they had stopped then, the community would never have known what it could become. Why stop now?

The first proposals were modest—improvements to housing, expansion of health services, investment in small-scale construction work that could employ Tribal members. But each suggestion sparked debate that lasted for hours, sometimes spilling into shouts. The wounds of the Pan American years had not healed. Suspicion shadowed every word.

The Crooks Legacy

The Crooks family, though quieter since Norm's removal, remained a presence. Some family members clung to the belief that outside managers were still necessary—that Indians could not run complex operations on their own. They echoed Norm's words: "Indians can't run these kinds of operations." To Leonard, it was not only defeatist but dangerous. It played into the same logic that had justified centuries of broken treaties and outside control.

He knew the only answer was to prove otherwise—through competence, transparency, and persistence. Each payroll met, each bill paid, each service delivered became its own rebuttal.

The National Debate

While Leonard fought local battles, the national debate over Indian gaming was escalating. In California, the Cabazon Band of Mission

Indians was locked in litigation with the state, a case that would eventually reach the Supreme Court. Across the country, states lobbied Congress to rein in Tribal gaming, arguing it was unregulated, untaxed, and unfair to state-run lotteries.

Shakopee, tiny as it was, found itself swept into the national story. Journalists noticed and started calling, curious how a small band of Dakota could operate high-stakes bingo just thirty miles from the Twin Cities. Lawmakers muttered about regulation. Pan American, still lurking in the industry, whispered that tribes couldn't handle things without professional managers.

Leonard understood the stakes. If Shakopee failed, it would not only confirm the doubters within the community but also fuel the arguments of those outside who sought to limit Tribal sovereignty nationwide. Their Little Six bingo hall was more than a local business—it was a test case in the court of public opinion.

Clashes at Home

Inside the community, the resistance was more personal. Council meetings became battlegrounds of philosophy. Leonard argued for reinvestment; others argued for larger per capita distributions. He wanted to build programs; they wanted immediate payouts.

The tension spilled into daily life. Family loyalties were tested. Parking lot confrontations flared again. Leonard carried himself with as much calm as he could muster, but he felt the strain. Every decision seemed to create as many enemies as allies.

And yet, amid the noise, there were signs of progress. The day care flourished. Housing programs slowly expanded. Basic accounting practices grew more disciplined. These were small steps, but to Leonard they were proof that the impossible might not be unreachable after all.

The Threshold of Transformation

The mid-1980s pressed hard on Leonard Prescott, but they also offered glimpses of promise. Each week still carried friction—council meetings thick with suspicion, debates over per capita distributions, and whispers of betrayal—but beneath the noise, the tribe was inching forward. Where once there had been only dependence on a management contract, there was now a growing sense of capacity. Programs were functioning, ledgers were balanced, and Tribal members were beginning to trust that operations could survive without outsiders pulling the strings.

Nationally, the stakes were rising. The Cabazon Band of Mission Indians, which had fought California over the right to operate high-stakes gaming on Tribal lands, in February 1987 received a favorable ruling by the United States Supreme Court. The decision confirmed what tribes had argued all along—gaming on Indian lands was a matter of Tribal sovereignty, not state control.

For Leonard, that decision was electric. It swept away the doubts that had lingered since Pan American's departure, doubts stoked by Norm Crooks' infamous declaration that "Indians can't run these kinds of operations." The Court had said otherwise. For the first time, the highest law of the land aligned with the lived struggle of a small Dakota community thirty miles from Minneapolis.

Fragile But Moving

At home, progress remained fragile. Some members saw the Cabazon decision as a green light for expansion. Others saw it as a reason for caution, warning that bigger risks could only magnify old divisions. Leonard often found himself alone at the center of those arguments, trying to balance the hunger for immediate per capita checks against the need to build long-term foundations.

Housing improvements moved forward in fits and starts. Health care expansions followed the same pattern—slow, piecemeal, often contentious. Yet each step was more than infrastructure; it was symbolic proof that Shakopee could use its revenues to serve its People. The community's day care and dental clinic became touchstones in community conversations, invoked as examples of what could be accomplished when money was reinvested rather than simply distributed.

Still, factionalism did not disappear. Parking lot fights occasionally flared again, and family grudges simmered just below the surface. Sovereignty, Leonard realized, was not a cure-all. It was a discipline, one that had to be renewed with every meeting, every decision, every payout.

The National Spotlight

As Shakopee stabilized, it attracted attention. More reporters were calling now, curious how such a tiny community had managed to pull itself free from a management contract and still run a profitable hall. Other tribes visited, eager to learn what worked and what didn't. The Bureau of Indian Affairs watched closely, as did state officials in Minnesota.

By 1987 and 1988, it was clear that Congress could not ignore the issue any longer. Tribes and Indian communities were operating high-stakes bingo and card games across the country, states were pressing for regulatory authority, and the gaming industry itself was circling with interest. The momentum of Cabazon had forced the federal government's hand. Hearings had begun in Washington, DC, laying the groundwork for what would become the Indian Gaming Regulatory Act (IGRA) of 1988.

For Leonard, the prospect of federal legislation was both hope and hazard. On one hand, IGRA promised to affirm what the Supreme Court had said—that tribes held the right to regulate gaming on their own lands. On the other, he knew Congress would try to build in restrictions, compromises, and oversight that could dull the edge of sovereignty.

A Larger Horizon

As he watched these national debates unfold, Leonard could not help but reflect on how far Shakopee had come. Only a few years earlier, they had been scraping together $1,500 from a grocer to keep the bingo hall open, begging for Brinks to quickly deliver cash for payouts, and fighting one another in parking lots. Now, they were part of a national story.

Leonard carried with him the lessons of those early days—the pain of betrayal, the humiliation of dependency, the slow but steady awakening of competence. Those memories gave weight to his vision. Economic growth was no longer just survival—it was a platform to reclaim dignity, restore culture, and build a government that could endure.

Leonard understood the irony well. The man who never wanted to be chairman now found himself at the center of a transformation not only for his community but for Indian Country as a whole. Shakopee was still small, still fragile, still prone to division. But with each month, each program, each reaffirmation of sovereignty, it was becoming something new.

What had begun as survival was turning into possibility. And possibility, if nurtured carefully, could become power.

To Washington and Beyond

Stepping into the National Arena

Leonard Prescott had not been chairman of the Shakopee Mdewakanton Sioux Community for long when his cousin Allene Ross pressed him into a decision. "Leonard," she said, "you're the chairman now, and you need to go to Washington and get involved in those issues that the national chairmen are involved in."

It was advice sharpened with realism. Some leaders seized power greedily, traveling constantly, chasing authority they didn't have. Allene assured Leonard she was no opportunist. While he was gone, she and the others on the council would hold the line. There would be no sudden changes, no surprise motions in his absence. The tribe would wait for his return.

So, in the winter of 1985, barely months into his tenure, Leonard boarded a plane bound for Washington, DC. It was his first business trip, farther than his boyhood dream of traveling to the Wisconsin Dells had ever taken him. He stepped off the plane into the cold air of the capital and walked into halls that had defined the lives of Native People for generations— the Cannon Building, the Rayburn Building, the Dirksen Building.

The architecture was meant to overwhelm—tall doors, marble corridors, ceilings arched like cathedrals of law. Leonard, thirty-four years old and untested on the national stage, carried in his heart the memory of his own community's poverty and the suspicions of families back home who doubted he could lead them through the storm.

The National Tribal Chairman's Association was his first stop. Chairmen from across Indian Country had come together to discuss education, economic development, health service shortfalls, and the impossible task of transforming scattered communities into modern governments. For Leonard, the meeting was an initiation. He listened more than he spoke, realizing that many of these men and women were already allied with the National Congress of American Indians (NCAI)—the most established Native voice in Washington, lobbying Congress directly and serving as watchdog against bills that chipped away at sovereignty.

Leonard remembered his first steps through those imposing halls of Congress, but what struck him most came later—the modest reality of Native advocacy. There was no grand office, no polished headquarters. The NCAI meetings took place in a rented housing unit, leaders gathered around card tables with potluck lunches spread between them. These were not men and women with corporate war chests; they were the stewards of fragile governments, scraping together money for airfare to protect their People's future.

The work, however, was heavy. The agenda was thick with budget concerns for the Interior Department, religious protection bills, and looming threats of federal interference in Tribal affairs. Chairmen spoke candidly about broken treaties, underfunded schools, and the constant risk of Congress taking more than it gave. Leonard realized that the questions he had wrestled with in Shakopee—the fairness of leadership, the distribution of resources, the danger of being exploited—were echoed everywhere.

In one of these meetings he met Josephine, a seasoned leader from Seattle who chaired with quiet authority. She admitted the Association had almost no stable funding, no permanent office, and no paid staff. Leonard thought of Shakopee. Fragile though his home community was, its high-stakes bingo revenues gave them something most tribes lacked—discretionary cash.

Standing in that crowded room, Leonard did something bold. He pledged $500,000 from Shakopee to support NCAI's administrative needs and lobbying work. It was a staggering sum for such a tiny community, but it bought the Association breathing room. Years later, Josephine would still thank him for that gesture: "You saved us in those early days."

This was Leonard's true education in sovereignty—not the abstract language of constitutions and petitions, but the living reality that sovereignty meant nothing if you lacked the means to defend it.

The Birth of NIGA

It was in this circle that Leonard met Manny Fierro, a sharp and seasoned representative of gaming tribes. Fierro explained that while NCAI fought on many fronts, tribes with bingo operations needed something more focused. Over coffee, he told Leonard of meetings already taking place in Florida. The Seminoles, pioneers of high-stakes bingo, had hosted a first gathering at the Eden Roc Hotel in Hollywood, Florida, drawing tribes who believed gaming was an inherent right of sovereignty—not a privilege to be granted by Congress.

A second meeting followed, also hosted by the Seminoles at the Eden Roc, where the talk turned more serious, aimed at forming an organization dedicated to defending gaming across Indian Country. Fierro invited Leonard into the next step.

The third gathering was held in Washington, DC, at the Marriott Hotel, hosted by the Fond du Lac Band of Lake Superior

Chippewa. There, the National Indian Gaming Association (NIGA) was officially created.

The slate of officers reflected the diversity and urgency of the movement. Billie Houle was elected chair, Joel Franks vice-chair, and Leonard Prescott—unexpectedly nominated by Houle himself—was chosen as secretary-treasurer. Around him were leaders from across the country: Billie Cypress, Percy Prowless, John James, Paul Nickels, Jerry Hill, Sharon House, Rita Kashena, Buzz Gutierrez, Josephine from Seattle, and representatives of the Morongo Band, among others.

Their mission was straightforward—defend high-stakes bingo, secure recognition of Tribal gaming rights, and act as a clearinghouse of information for tribes facing hostile legislatures and skeptical courts.

But Leonard had a narrower and even more burning question. Would video games of chance—the machines slowly filling Las Vegas casinos—be included in any federal Indian gaming bill? He pressed the issue at every opportunity, knowing that the survival of gaming as a true engine of economic independence might hinge on that single question.

Allies and Opponents

The formation of the National Indian Gaming Association came at a moment when Congress was sharpening its knives. There were powerful voices arrayed against Tribal gaming. Legislators such as Representative Tony Coelho, Representative Slade Gorton, and Nevada's Senator Harry Reid warned of chaos if tribes were allowed to operate gaming enterprises free from state control. Their message was simple: "No gaming on reservations." Behind them were the interests of Las Vegas, Atlantic City, and state governments wary of losing tax revenue to sovereign Nations inside their borders.

But there were also allies—stalwart defenders who understood both the injustices of history and the opportunities gaming presented. Chief among them was Senator Daniel Inouye of Hawaii, a war hero who carried scars from World War II and from a lifetime of prejudice against Japanese Americans. He chaired the Senate Select Committee on Indian Affairs, and his presence gave the tribes not just a champion, but a man who knew, in his bones, the weight of exclusion.

On the House side, Representative George Miller of California, serving on the House Interior and Insular Affairs Committee, pushed back against efforts to strip tribes of control. Miller's voice was plain and consistent—Indian gaming was not a loophole. It was a right rooted in sovereignty.

This was the battlefield Leonard had stepped into—committee rooms, rented halls, and late-night meetings where allies and enemies alike mapped the future of Indian Country.

A Clearinghouse of Sovereignty

NIGA's first mission was survival. "Save high-stakes bingo and get whatever else we can salvage," as one elder chairman bluntly put it. The Association acted as a clearinghouse of information, gathering reports from gaming tribes and warning others of legislative moves that threatened sovereignty.

Each meeting carried a sense of urgency. Some Tribal leaders came from states openly hostile to Native rights; others from states with lukewarm or "mildly supportive" attitudes. Yet their struggles converged. Whether Seminole in Florida, Morongo in California, or Mdewakanton in Minnesota, the questions were the same: How do we protect our games? How do we keep Congress from caging us in regulations meant to control us rather than help us thrive?

Leonard, the youngest officer in the room, kept reminding himself that a few years earlier he had been uncertain of his own cultural grounding, torn between urban life and reservation politics. Now he sat at the table where tribes mapped out strategy for the next generation.

The Eden Roc Gatherings

The Seminoles of Florida had already proven that high-stakes bingo could transform a Tribal Nation. By 1979, their hall outside Fort Lauderdale was a financial marvel, and the New England Entertainment Company—later known as Pan American Gaming—had built its reputation on Seminole success. Now, in 1984 and 1985, the Seminoles hosted something new—gatherings of Tribal leaders to discuss not just games, but sovereignty itself.

The venue was the Eden Roc Hotel in Hollywood, Florida, a glamorous oceanfront landmark with art-deco bones and the faint smell of saltwater drifting through its lobbies. For many Tribal leaders—men and women who had grown up in cinderblock homes on underfunded reservations—the hotel was almost surreal. Crystal chandeliers, mirrored hallways, white-suited attendants who nodded as though all guests were royalty. It was a reminder that Indian Country was stepping onto a national stage where perception mattered as much as principle.

Leonard was not present at the first meeting, but by the second gathering, word had spread far and wide. Manny Fierro, energetic and tireless, had begun pulling together tribes who knew that their bingo halls were under siege. "This is bigger than bingo," Fierro told them. "This is about the right to decide for ourselves. If they can take bingo, they can take everything."

Breakout sessions filled the Eden Roc's ballrooms. Seminole hosts offered hospitality with quiet pride, reminding their guests that it was Seminole defiance—and their court victory against Florida officials—that had cracked open the door for all. Delegates traded stories—the Cabazon Band in California, already locked in lawsuits with Riverside County; the Morongo Band, facing similar harassment; northern tribes in Wisconsin and Minnesota watching state legislatures circle like hawks.

It was at Eden Roc that the idea of a National Indian Gaming Association took its first real shape. The conversations were raw, sometimes chaotic. Some leaders feared Congress might outlaw gaming altogether if tribes pushed too hard. Others argued that unity was the only shield strong enough to resist. A small drafting group began sketching out bylaws for an association that would monitor legislation, lobby Congress, and most importantly, proclaim sovereignty as the legal and moral ground on which Tribal gaming stood.

Fond du Lac and Formal Birth

Momentum carried into the third meeting, hosted by the Fond du Lac Band of Lake Superior Chippewa, this time in Washington, DC, at the Marriott Hotel. The Eden Roc glamour was gone. Here, the halls were filled with congressional aides, lobbyists, and journalists sniffing at a new story about "Indian gambling."

In that setting, the National Indian Gaming Association (NIGA) was officially born in the spring of 1985. Officers were elected: Billie Houle as chair, Joel Frank as vice-chair, and Leonard—still barely settled into his role as Shakopee chairman—nominated by Houle to serve as secretary-treasurer. The vote was swift, the confidence unmistakable.

For Leonard, it was dizzying. He had been chairman of SMSC for such a short time. Now he was suddenly responsible not just for his tiny community in Minnesota, but for helping manage an association that represented dozens of sovereign Nations across the country. He carried a notebook in those days, scribbling names: Billie Cypress, Percy Prowless, John James, Paul Nickels, Jerry

Hill, Sharon House, Rita Kashena, Buzz Gutierrez, Josephine from Seattle, the Morongo representatives from California. He knew he could not afford to forget a single ally.

The meetings were still humble. There was no Washington office, no polished staff. They rented modest spaces, ate potluck lunches, and pooled meager funds. Leonard remembered offering $500,000 from Shakopee's bingo revenues—an astonishing sum at the time—to help sustain the Association's early lobbying efforts. "We had to show them we were serious," he later reflected. "If sovereignty was worth anything, it was worth investing in."

The Shape of Opposition

No sooner had NIGA been born than its enemies pressed harder. Congressional hearings echoed with warnings about organized crime, gambling addiction, and the supposed dangers of "unregulated Indian casinos." State attorneys general lobbied for preemption, insisting that only states could be trusted to police gambling.

Yet, Leonard and his peers knew the truth—states were not neutral referees. They were competitors, jealous of revenues and unwilling to cede authority to tribes. To let states control Indian gaming would be to surrender sovereignty itself.

The names of opponents became a familiar litany—Coelho, Gorton, Reid. The allies stood like pillars—Inouye in the Senate, Miller in the House. Each side understood what was at stake. For tribes, it was nothing less than survival, a chance to escape cycles of poverty and dependence. For opponents, it was a question of who held power in America's gambling economy.

Back to Shakopee

When Leonard returned home after these national meetings, the contrast could not have been sharper. In Washington, he had walked through the Dirksen, Rayburn, and Cannon Buildings, past brass nameplates and the echo of marble corridors. In Shakopee, the reality was far humbler—a corrugated metal bingo hall, a divided community, and nightly disputes over where the money went.

Still, he felt the connection. "What we decide here," he told his council, "will echo in Washington. And what we win there will decide whether we have a future here."

The irony was not lost on him. Shakopee was one of the smallest tribes in the nation, just over a dozen charter members. Yet because of its proximity to the Twin Cities and the stubbornness of its People, it now had a voice in shaping a national movement.

And so Leonard Prescott, once unsure of his cultural grounding, now found himself standing between two worlds—the stormy parking lots of Shakopee and the polished chambers of Capitol Hill. Both demanded his full attention. Both would test his resolve.

Sparks in Silicon – Video Games of Chance

It began, as breakthroughs often do, with a small lunch and a bigger question. In roughly March of 1985, Leonard's sister Pat struck up conversations with Mary Sue Kiland, whose family business supplied bars and other venues with gaming entertainment devices. Mary Sue had an idea. What if Shakopee tried her machines in the newly built Little Six Bingo Lounge—a limited trial, sovereign land meeting new technology. After an initial talk, Leonard and Pat met again with Mary Sue and her father, John Kiland, to run hard numbers—profitability, lease terms, and, crucially, how the tribe's sovereign status could unlock a gaming opportunity the state could neither tax nor easily restrain.

Leonard carried that proposal across the hallway to Bob Page and the Tribal offices. His pitch was simple and pointed—install thirty machines as a pilot, learn fast, then scale if the data supported it. A deal took shape—a 70/30 revenue split with Kiland after expenses. A small marketing flier was sent out. The machines were rolling in within days.

The Kiland devices were not slot machines in the old Vegas sense—no chrome handles, no whirring reels, no buckets of coins.

These cabinets used random number generators. Players pressed buttons rather than pulling levers. Payouts emerged as printed tickets that could be redeemed for cash at the cage. The difference sounded technical, but on the floor it felt transformative. Player response was immediate. Players learned the rhythm fast, and the bingo crowd—already primed for numbers, patterns, and near-miss thrills—took to the new format with startling enthusiasm.

Success begets scale. The tribe ordered another hundred machines, and those too found their audience. With cash flow rising, Leonard and Pat circled back to the Kilands. The pilot had done its job. Now the tribe's leverage was real, so Leonard pressed for better economics on the original 70/30 split.

Word traveled—farther and faster than anyone expected. "Slot machines on an Indian reservation" became not just a rumor but a headline, a talking point in county meetings, then a curiosity in neighboring states, and soon a topic of national interest. That attention drew a new suitor—an Austrian manufacturer, the Novamatic Gaming Company, invited Shakopee to view its product line at its corporate headquarters overseas. Leonard couldn't get away, but Pat could. She took Angie, Leonard's wife, and they flew to Austria.

From across the Atlantic came upbeat reports. Angie called home with running commentary about the tour of Novamatic's casino, a walkthrough of its machine shop, demonstrations of cabinet reliability and game variety—everything Shakopee needed to help the community bargain down lease rates and diversify the floor.

When Pat and Angie returned, Leonard greenlit an order for one hundred Novamatic machines. Installation crews arrived and went to work. On the strength of Shakopee's newfound leverage, the Kiland Company agreed to drop its take to 15 percent. The tribe launched a Grand Opening to showcase the new lineup—Novamatic cabinets standing alongside the legacy Kiland devices that had kick-started the experiment. As a bonus, Shakopee's already innovative Bingo Jack and Bingo Roulette tables were present, offering games similar to bingo yet played on a Vegas-like blackjack or craps table with bingo balls.

What looked on paper like a procurement decision was in truth a strategic hinge—technology, sovereignty, and market timing aligning like the symbols on a Vegas slot machine. Leonard's approach ran on two rails. First, he took an active national role when he helped found the National Indian Gaming Association and becoming its secretary–treasurer in September 1985 to protect the policy space tribes needed. Second, he engaged in face-to-face retail politics by personally pressing key legislators to embrace not only high-stakes bingo but video games of chance. If Shakopee's machines were the spark, the federal law would be the oxygen.

Those lobbying rounds were not always in step with the priorities of other tribes, however. Many high-stakes bingo leaders focused on guarding bingo itself and preserving state charitable games from being outlawed by overbroad federal fixes. Leonard agreed with that near-term defense but insisted on a second objective—to *grandfather in* video games of chance already operating at Shakopee, then create a pathway for all Minnesota Tribal governments.

From 1985 through 1987, draft after draft of Indian gaming bills surfaced and stalled. Most were too constricting. Still, visibility grew. The reality of gaming on reservations could no longer be ignored.

Then came the legal thunderclap mentioned earlier. In 1987, the U.S. Supreme Court decided the case brought by California against the Cabazon Band of Mission Indians, in which the state had tried to cap jackpots under its charitable limits. The Court sided with Cabazon. Tribes, as separate sovereigns, possessed their own civil–regulatory authority, according to the Supreme Court. Because bingo was a civil-regulatory matter—not criminal—tribes could operate it under their own rules, not the state's charity-law ceiling (so often around $500 at the time).

Overnight, a door opened—and with it, a stampede of anxiety. Las Vegas and Atlantic City interests, state attorneys general, the charitable gaming industry, the National Governors Association, and a constellation of others realized tribes might lawfully operate gaming nationwide without state or federal micromanagement. Panic followed, with millions pouring into lobbying to curtail or channel Tribal rights.

Leonard read the moment clearly. Congress, rattled by Cabazon but unable to stuff the genie back into the bottle, would try to codify a framework that would allow Tribal gaming—especially bingo—while limiting expansion into full casino-style games unless states retained leverage.

Through 1987 and into 1988, "trial balloon" bills rose and sank. As the 1988 session ran short in October, Leonard doubled down on Minnesota's interests. He met repeatedly with Senator Rudy Boschwitz, one of Minnesota's two Republican senators, who was then campaigning for a second term. A critical meeting landed at the Minnesota State Fair the weekend before the Senate's September 17, 1988 vote. Leonard made the case to Senator Boschwitz with no varnish—video games of chance were the financial spine of Minnesota's Tribal future.

On the Senate floor, Boschwitz pressed the point and collided with Senator Harry Reid of Nevada, whose loyalty to the Vegas industry was a matter of record. Boschwitz argued for time and space—Minnesota tribes already offered video games, and their economic development depended on them.

Reid offered a hard-edged compromise: Video games of chance could be allowed if tribes entered compacts with their states, with a one-year deadline for negotiations. Further, any tribe operating gaming two years prior to enactment would be grandfathered for one year to obtain a compact. The language nodded toward national parity but, in practice, and as a nod to Boschwitz, recognized Minnesota's situation. No other tribes—and no other states—were then running the same video game footprint as the Mdewakanton community in Shakopee. In effect, the carve-out was exclusive to Minnesota.

Leonard didn't blink. If that was the path, he would walk it fast. He began coordinating across all eleven tribes in Minnesota, a diplomatic gesture by any measure. Shakopee, with barely one hundred members at the time and a land base of only 250.8 acres, had rarely been granted a loud voice in statewide Tribal politics. Larger Nations—especially the Minnesota Chippewa communities under a shared constitutional umbrella—were accustomed to leading. Pride mattered. But so did protocol. No chairman wanted to be seen taking direction from another chairman. Still, success speaks. Shakopee's results had turned curiosity into respect. A sliver of leverage opened.

Leonard worked the phones, drove the miles, and sat through late-night meetings where skepticism softened by inches. He argued not for Shakopee's advantage but for a shared future—compacts as the legal bridge, video games as the revenue engine, unity as the shield.

On the very last day of Minnesota's one-year window—October 17, 1989—Leonard Prescott secured signed compacts with six tribes. Then came welcome news from Washington. Senator Reid had agreed to a one-year extension. With time reset, Leonard finished the circuit. In the end, all eleven tribes signed video game compacts. What began as a modest pilot—thirty machines at a 70/30 split—had become a statewide framework and a national precedent—technology + sovereignty + unity welded under pressure into policy.

An aerial view of a portion of the snowy SMSC reservation in 1989 showing Little Six Bingo.

Looking back, the sequence reads like a straight line.

Meet the Kilands.

1. Install the first machines.
2. Prove the model.
3. Press terms down to 15 percent.
4. Fly to Austria.
5. Bring in Novamatic.
6. Launch Grand Opening beside Bingo Jack and Bingo Roulette.
7. Fight in DC.
8. Ride the shockwaves of Cabazon.
9. Stand with Boschwitz against Reid.
10. Accept the compact bargain.
11. And then, one by one, ink Minnesota's signatures.

In the moment, however, it felt nothing like a straight line. It felt like triage and audacity—making policy with one hand and clearing jammed ticket printers with the other—held together by a stubborn conviction that tribes could invent their way out of historical scarcity if given even a narrow lane.

Innovation wasn't only silicon and buttons. It was also the political circuitry Leonard had been soldering since his first trip to the Rayburn and Dirksen buildings—the belief that sovereignty is lived in the particulars of lease percentages, compact deadlines, machine mix, floor layout, and the names on the bill. And that when tribes stand together, a sliver of daylight can become a corridor wide enough for a People to walk through.

The $8.8 Million Loan

In the gaming business, vigilance was a necessity. Leonard Prescott knew enough from his tribe's entanglement with Pan American Gaming to recognize that the path of sudden prosperity was also the path where underworld figures lurked. Shakopee's sovereignty and its new-found revenues made it a target. Every deal, every handshake, required discernment.

That was why he valued Bob Page. Page was no Tribal member, but he was no hustler either. Born and raised in Prior Lake, a faithful Catholic, a family man, and once an insurance salesman, he had stepped into Shakopee's world of high-stakes bingo as a steady hand. Leonard described him simply: "Bob and his family were the epitome of honesty and good judgment." In a period when trust was a rare commodity, Leonard trusted Page.

It was to Page, then, that Leonard turned when the idea of a federal loan first surfaced. Page had gone to college with Senator David Durenberger, the Republican from Minnesota. Leonard asked for a favor: Would Page call on his old classmate and see if the senator might hear out Shakopee's case for a 90 percent loan guarantee through the Department of the Interior?

Page agreed. The request was made. And, in a surprising but providential turn, Senator Durenberger responded. After reviewing the tribe's proposal, he agreed that the project—a casino on Indian trust land, backed by a solid market study—deserved serious consideration. He arranged for a face-to-face meeting in Washington, DC.

The Third Meeting

It was not the first attempt. By the spring of 1985, Leonard and Bob had already sat through two hesitant, fruitless meetings with Interior officials. Their proposal had been laid out in full—a request for a $13.6 million loan, payable in five years, supported by market data projecting strong profitability. Yet each time, the Bureau had balked.

The objections were couched in the language of fairness. Shakopee was small—barely 300 members at the time, with only 250 acres of land. The Bureau's annual loan guarantee allocation totaled $45 million, and of that, only $14 million remained. How could such a tiny tribe justify consuming nearly the entire balance?

To Eddie Brown, the assistant secretary of Indian affairs, the request bordered on ludicrous. Approving such a loan might also open the floodgates. Other tribes could demand the same treatment, and soon the department would be underwriting casinos across Indian Country.

But on the third try, Senator Durenberger himself came to the table.

The meeting room symbolized the imbalance. Eddie Brown and his assistant Veronica Murdock sat at the head of a long sixteen-foot table. Leonard and Bob occupied the far, opposite end—distant, almost ceremonially. Senator Durenberger took a seat near the secretary, his presence instantly shifting the gravity of the room.

Leonard spoke first. He kept it brief, reiterating the profitability study, the tribe's repayment plan, and a striking statistic: 90 percent of all guaranteed loans at the time were in default. Shakopee's plan, he argued, was different. It could not only succeed, but perhaps even pay ahead of schedule.

Brown asked a few questions. Leonard answered them evenly. Then Durenberger leaned forward.

Durenberger's Pressure

The Senator's questions cut straight to the hesitation that had plagued the Bureau. Was there a hard policy cap at $3 million, as officials had suggested in earlier meetings? Brown admitted there was not. Was the risk of default higher than the potential? Brown conceded that this proposal appeared unusually strong. Finally, Durenberger asked the bluntest question of all. Did the secretary personally believe the Shakopee project would succeed? Brown said yes.

That was the opening. Durenberger's tone sharpened. "I have three minutes left in this meeting," he said flatly. "Are you going to do what you are supposed to do for a tribe in the way of economic development—a tribe that intends to pay the money back in five years? Or do we have to do this in Congress?"

The room went silent. The assistant secretary fumbled. His face hardened into bureaucratic caution, but he could not escape the corner.

Finally, he relented. "Senator, we have reviewed the proposal by Shakopee for a casino, and we agree that a loan can be paid back. We can give them $8.8 million in a 90 percent guarantee loan."

The Whisper

Durenberger turned to Leonard. "Mr. Chairman, would $8.8 million be sufficient?"

Before Leonard could answer, Bob Page leaned close, cupped his hand to his mouth, and whispered loud enough for all to hear: "Take it."

Leonard nodded. "Yes, Senator. That will be sufficient."

The secretary gestured toward his assistant. "Mr. Chairman, since we have a deal, this is my assistant, Veronica Murdock. If you have any problems going forth, she will take full responsibility for moving us forward."

They stood and shook hands. Durenberger offered congratulations. The meeting ended not with ceremony but with a sense of astonishment. Against all odds, the smallest of tribes had secured millions in federal backing.

Leonard walked out of the Interior building in awe. For a People long dismissed as irrelevant, for a reservation once defined by poverty and factional strife, this was a breakthrough that felt almost impossible. It echoed the moment when the Indian Gaming Regulatory Act had passed: the sense that survival was no longer in question, that sovereignty had substance.

He understood the secretary's calculus. The full $13.6 million had been out of reach. But $8.8 million—earmarked for building construction and materials—was enough to lay the foundation. What the Bureau refused to cover—furniture, fixtures, slot machines—Shakopee would have to finance elsewhere.

The irony was sharp. This would be the first and only Tribal economic development loan ever granted for a casino. No tribe before or since would receive such support. For Shakopee, it meant possibility beyond imagination. For Leonard, it meant responsibility bordering on unbearable.

"To say I had my hands full was a gross understatement," he later admitted. "Now I could afford to build the casino. But little did I know what would lie ahead."

The announcement of the loan rippled through Shakopee like thunder across the valley. For years, the community had lived in the shadow of limited means, arguing over pennies and burdened by mistrust. Now, with the stroke of a pen, millions of dollars had been promised. It was more money than the tribe had ever imagined seeing at once, and its implications were staggering.

Some members celebrated. They spoke of new jobs, better housing, and the dignity of knowing Shakopee would no longer beg for scraps from the Bureau of Indian Affairs. Others whispered suspicions. Had Leonard made a devil's bargain in Washington? Would this money come with strings they could not see?

The tension was not unfamiliar. Every step forward seemed to divide the community, just as the breakup with Pan American had split families and friendships. Leonard felt the old doubts creeping in. Yet he also knew that this time was different. This was not a management company's contract or a personal side deal like Norm Crooks had engineered. This was the United States government, acknowledging—if only begrudgingly—that Shakopee had the right and the capacity to stand on its own feet.

A New Kind of Responsibility

The $8.8 million loan guarantee was both blessing and burden. Construction of a casino was no longer a dream whispered in council meetings or floated in speculative proposals. It was a reality that had to be managed with precision.

Leonard quickly realized the loan only covered part of what was needed. The Bureau had been deliberate in its exclusions—bricks and mortar, yes. Slot machines, fixtures, and furnishings, no. The tribe would have to find creative financing for those, navigating lenders who had long dismissed Shakopee as too small, too unstable, or too risky.

That meant more meetings, more negotiations, more sleepless nights. Every dollar had to be accounted for. Every expenditure had to be justified. The stakes were no longer theoretical. If Shakopee faltered now, it would not just be embarrassment, it would be default, and the end of credibility for years to come.

Rising in Washington

The loan also changed Leonard's stature nationally. No longer was Shakopee dismissed as a curiosity, a "tiny tribe with a bingo hall." Other Tribal leaders began asking questions. How had he persuaded Senator Durenberger to lean so hard on the Bureau? What was the secret? Could it be replicated?

Leonard knew there was no secret—only persistence, data, and the right allies at the right moment. Yet he also knew that Shakopee's success put it in a precarious place. Larger tribes, particularly the Minnesota Chippewa bands under one constitutional umbrella, resented the idea that a community of barely three hundred members could suddenly wield influence. Some feared Shakopee's victory would provoke a backlash, jeopardizing all of Indian Country's progress in gaming.

But in Washington, the tide was shifting. The Indian Gaming Regulatory Act was now a live debate. Legislators who once ignored tribes could no longer afford to do so. And Shakopee's story—the tiny Nation that had leveraged sovereignty and persistence into a multi-million-dollar loan—was proof of what was possible.

Back Home

Back on the reservation, the contrast was sharp. Members still lived in modest homes, some in trailers, some without reliable plumbing. Arguments still broke out in the parking lot of the bingo hall. Old wounds still festered.

Yet, even amid the turmoil, there was a new undercurrent. For the first time, people spoke of a future not in terms of survival, but in terms of possibility. The casino project promised jobs, services, and revenue streams that could finally support dreams beyond subsistence.

Leonard carried that weight with him. "To say I had my hands full was a gross understatement," he often reflected. But he also understood that this was the moment when history bent. Shakopee, once on the margins of Indian Country, was now at the center of a storm that would reshape Native sovereignty and American gaming alike.

Breaking Ground

The winter of 1991 bled into spring with a nervous energy. Surveyors arrived, then architects, then contractors in hard hats who paced the bare ground with clipboards and rolled blueprints. For decades, the Shakopee lands had been quiet—patches of farmland, woods, and a scattering of homes. Now bulldozers cut deep into the earth. Foundations were poured. Trucks rattled across gravel, kicking dust into the sky.

To an outsider, it was ordinary construction. To the community, it was astonishing—the first casino on sovereign Shakopee soil, financed not by a management company siphoning off profits, but by a federal loan guarantee wrestled into existence through grit and political persuasion.

Some families came to watch daily, standing at the fence lines. Children asked questions. Elders shook their heads in disbelief. A few muttered warnings about the dangers of money and outsiders. Others whispered prayers of thanks.

The Practical Burden

The $8.8 million loan covered concrete, steel, roofing, plumbing—everything needed to raise walls and create a functioning building. But it did not cover the soul of the enterprise—the games themselves. Slot machines, tables, décor, lighting—the things that would attract and hold players—all were outside the scope of the loan.

Leonard and the council had to scramble. They negotiated with vendors, leased machines, leaned on relationships built during the bingo years. Every purchase was a balancing act. A grand chandelier for the lobby meant fewer machines on the floor. A better ventilation system meant cutting corners elsewhere.

Leonard often stayed up late, running numbers with Bob Page, his trusted bingo manager. They scribbled on yellow legal pads, debating whether to lease more machines or buy them outright. "Every decision we make now," Leonard told Page one night, "will decide whether this thing sinks us or saves us."

The Weight of Scrutiny

The project did not go unnoticed. Newspapers in Minneapolis and St. Paul sent reporters to cover the "reservation casino." Editorials warned of crime, addiction, and mob infiltration. Politicians sniffed at the idea of a tiny tribe building an enterprise that the state itself could not control.

At the national level, lobbyists for Las Vegas and Atlantic City circulated memos in Congress. If Shakopee succeeded, they argued, it would be the first domino. Other tribes would follow. Soon Indian Country would be filled with casinos, siphoning billions away from established gaming industries and state tax bases.

That was precisely Leonard's point. For the first time in generations, tribes had a tool to lift themselves from poverty without asking permission from state governments that had long exploited them. But the louder he spoke, the sharper the opposition grew.

Inside the Community

The noise outside was matched by friction within. Old rivalries resurfaced. Some families accused Leonard of chasing glory in Washington while leaving daily disputes unresolved at home. Others feared the casino would widen gaps between those with influence and those without.

Parking lot arguments flared again, this time about construction contracts, hiring priorities, and rumors of payoffs. Leonard tried to remain calm, reminding everyone that this was their collective chance, their shared project. Yet he knew the truth. Sovereignty meant nothing if the community could not govern itself with fairness and discipline.

Still, he pressed on. "This isn't just about games," he told a crowded general council meeting. "It's about proving we can build something ourselves—without being cheated, without being managed, without being told we're too small to matter."

The Building Takes Shape

By late summer, steel beams framed the sky. Walls went up, followed by insulation and siding. Electricians wired circuits, plumbers connected lines. Every day brought new progress.

The building itself was modest compared to the glitter of Las Vegas, but to Shakopee it felt monumental—a physical symbol of survival and possibility. It was the first casino financed directly under the federal loan guarantee program. The *only* one, as it would turn out.

Leonard walked the site often, hard hat on his head, boots kicking through sawdust. He would stop to speak with workers, some of them Tribal members, others contractors from nearby towns. He reminded them—sometimes with pride, sometimes with urgency—that this project was more than a job. "This is our future," he would say.

Preparing for the Opening

By the spring of 1992, the building stood nearly complete. Fresh paint covered the walls, carpets stretched across the gaming floor, and the smell of new upholstery hung in the air. Crews tested lights and checked wiring. Trucks delivered slot machines under heavy tarps, guarded as though they were sacred cargo.

The council debated endlessly over details—the placement of machines, the size of the cashier's cage, even the design of the front sign. Some members wanted grandeur, a building that announced sovereignty to every visitor. Others counseled caution—better to start modest, prove success, and expand later.

Leonard listened to every argument but always returned to the same refrain: "This is our first step, not our last. We build it solid, we build it honest, and the future will take care of itself."

Marketing was another challenge. Unlike the bingo hall, which had drawn locals with flyers and word of mouth, the casino needed a larger reach. Ads were placed in Twin Cities papers. Radio spots promised excitement "closer than you think." Rumors spread quickly. Bus companies called, asking if they could schedule runs. The buzz grew louder by the week.

The Grand Opening

On a crisp October morning, cars lined the gravel road leading to the reservation. Buses pulled in, brakes hissing, unloading eager gamblers from Minneapolis, St. Paul, even Chicago. The parking lot filled faster than anyone had anticipated.

Inside, the air was electric. The hum of machines blended with the chatter of hundreds of voices. Dealers shuffled cards at blackjack tables. Lights blinked across rows of slots. The cashier's line stretched long as people clutched their first tickets and winnings.

Leonard walked the floor, trying to take it all in. For a moment, he felt like he was watching history bend in real time. Elders who had grown up in poverty now leaned against polished counters, shaking their heads in disbelief. Younger members worked as dealers, cashiers, attendants—their first real jobs on sovereign ground.

The press had come too. Reporters scribbled notes, cameras flashed. Some stories were skeptical, others outright hostile, painting the casino as an "experiment" or a "threat." But to Leonard, the images of Tribal members working, earning, and standing proud outweighed every headline.

National Reverberations

The opening was more than a local event—it rippled across Indian Country and beyond. Other tribes called, asking about contracts, about financing, about machines. Lawyers and lobbyists studied the details of the $8.8 million loan, already strategizing how to replicate—or prevent—another big loan.

In Washington, congressional staffers noted the turnout and revenue figures. The Shakopee casino, tiny by Las Vegas standards, was nonetheless proof that Tribal gaming could generate real profit. That fact unsettled governors, attorneys general, and gaming executives across the country.

The whispers grew: *If Shakopee could do it, anyone could.*

The Cost of Success

But success carried weight. The loan still had to be repaid. Machines had to be maintained, employees trained, books balanced. Every day brought new challenges—disputes over payouts, complaints about smoke, the need for tighter security.

Within the community, tensions simmered. Some families wanted larger per capita distributions immediately. Others insisted the money should go to housing, education, health care. Old suspicions resurfaced—who was really in charge, and who was benefiting most?

Leonard bore it all with a mix of determination and exhaustion. "We asked for this," he reminded the council. "We fought for it, and now it's ours. That means we have to prove we can handle it."

Looking back, Leonard would see the grand opening as the true turning point. The Little Six bingo hall had been a prelude, an introduction. The loan fight had been a battle of words and signatures. But the casino's first night of operation was something else entirely—the moment when Shakopee stepped onto a stage from which it could never retreat.

The doors of Mystic Lake had opened, the games had begun, and the world was watching.

The First Numbers

Within weeks, the numbers were staggering. Daily reports crossed Leonard's desk showing revenue far beyond the council's most optimistic projections. Cash drawers overflowed, tickets piled high, and the cashier's cage required reinforcement simply to handle the constant flow.

By the end of the first quarter, repayment of the $8.8 million loan was already underway. What had once seemed like an audacious gamble now looked almost conservative. Economists later marveled at the speed with which the debt shrank, but for Leonard, it was more than a financial story: It was vindication—that sovereignty, wisely exercised, could transform lives.

The state took notice too. Newspaper editorials warned of "unchecked Indian gambling." Politicians muttered about the need for oversight. But those same critics could not deny that the Mdewakanton had pulled off something unprecedented—a small community, barely recognized a decade earlier and nonexistent decades before that, had harnessed gaming to create genuine wealth.

New Responsibilities

With success came new responsibilities. The council debated endlessly—what to build first, how much to distribute, how to balance individual needs against community priorities. Elders called for better housing. Young parents demanded new schools and childcare. Some simply wanted their share in hand, tired of poverty and sacrifice.

Leonard walked a tightrope. Too much per capita distribution could starve long-term development. Too little could fracture the fragile trust he had built. He urged patience, reminding members that true sovereignty meant building institutions—health clinics, cultural centers, education funds—that would outlast any one generation.

Not everyone agreed. Parking lot arguments persisted, sometimes escalating into shoving matches as patrons filed past to gamble. The glow of the casino's success had not erased old wounds within the community.

The Human Side of Success

For Leonard, the transformation was personal. He remembered his childhood in poverty, the doubts about his identity, the years of struggle with Angie's illness, the humiliation of being dismissed as "just another Prescott." Now, as chairman, he signed checks that funded scholarships, housing improvements, and health care programs.

He also knew the danger of arrogance. Each time he walked the casino floor, he reminded himself—*This is not mine. This is theirs—the community's. I am only the steward.*

That humility earned him respect from some, suspicion from others. But it kept him grounded as new opportunities and new temptations crowded in.

A Wider Horizon

The casino's success amplified Shakopee's voice nationally. Tribes from across the country called Leonard, asking for advice.

Lobbyists sought him out in Washington, eager to secure his support. Newspapers profiled the "tiny tribe with a big casino," alternately praising and criticizing what they saw as a new kind of Indian story.

In the halls of Congress, the debate over Indian gaming sharpened. The success in Shakopee became Exhibit A for both sides. Supporters pointed to jobs created, debts repaid, services funded. Opponents warned of a "wildfire" that could sweep the country if every tribe followed suit.

Through it all, Leonard carried the weight of knowing that his community's future—and perhaps the future of Indian gaming itself—was being judged by every dollar that passed across the cashier's counter.

By the end of the first year, the loan repayment schedule was far ahead of plan. The council began drafting blueprints for expansion—more machines, more tables, better facilities. Yet Leonard never forgot the tension in that Washington meeting when the assistant secretary hesitated, or the urgency in Senator Durenberger's voice when he demanded action.

The $8.8 million loan had not just built a casino. It had built a stage—one on which the Shakopee Mdewakanton Sioux Community would play a leading role in the national story of Tribal sovereignty, gaming, and survival.

And Leonard, once a reluctant chairman, now found himself the face of a movement far larger than he had ever imagined.

Scrutiny from the Outside

As the projects took shape—houses, clinics, scholarships, cultural centers—the outside world began to notice. For decades, Shakopee had been regarded as little more than a footnote in Minnesota history—a small, obscure Dakota community on a patch of marginal land. Now, reporters drove down County Road 42 with cameras and notebooks, asking how a tribe of barely a hundred people could suddenly fund developments that neighboring towns struggled to afford.

Local politicians also took notice. County commissioners wondered aloud about "unfair advantages," pointing to Shakopee's tax-exempt status. State legislators muttered that gambling revenues should be shared more broadly, perhaps taxed or regulated. In Saint Paul, a few even suggested that the tribe's sovereignty ought to be reexamined in light of its new prosperity.

Leonard had anticipated this. Across Indian Country, he had seen that whenever tribes gained even a modest foothold of wealth, outsiders sought to cut it back. "They never come for you when you're poor," he told the council. "It's only when you stand up that they remember your name."

The Media Narrative

The media added fuel to all opinions. Articles in Minneapolis and Saint Paul papers alternated between fascination and suspicion. Some stories praised the tribe's success, noting how gaming revenues were funding health, housing, and education. Others played into stereotypes, hinting at corruption or waste. Headlines often emphasized the small size of the community, as though prosperity was illegitimate unless shared with outsiders.

Reporters asked about Leonard personally. Who was this young chairman steering the tribe from obscurity into national headlines? Some described him as charismatic, others as controversial. Their portrayal of him, as always, depended on who was interviewed. Leonard's opponents in the community rarely missed an opportunity to cast doubt.

Neighbors and Envy

The tribe's immediate neighbors also reacted. Residents in Prior Lake and Shakopee, once indifferent to the community across the highway, began to look with a mix of envy and resentment. They saw new houses rising on trust land, unburdened by property taxes. They saw cars with shiny new plates in the bingo hall parking lot. And they asked, some perhaps with a touch of innate bias: Why should Indians have what we don't?

Leonard knew these sentiments well. They were echoes of the old hostility that had driven the Dakota from their lands in the first place. What had once been contempt for poverty was now suspicion of success. Either way, the tribe could not win in the eyes of some neighbors.

State and Federal Maneuvers

In the statehouse, legislators began drafting "study bills" to examine Indian gaming. These were usually thinly veiled attempts to assert control over the thriving Mdewakanton. Lobbyists for Las Vegas and Atlantic City operators made quiet calls, warning that Tribal casinos might siphon revenue from established gambling centers. Attorneys general from other states whispered about lawsuits, seeking test cases to curtail sovereignty.

The pressure was no less in Washington. Though Leonard had allies like Senator Inouye and Representative George Miller, there were also entrenched opponents. Nevada's Harry Reid, loyal to the casino industry, reasserted his opposition to the unchecked expansion of Indian gaming. Every gain at Shakopee seemed to draw sharper questions in committee hearings.

Internal Pressure

Even within the tribe, pressure mounted. Some members argued that more of the revenue should go directly into per capita payments to SMSC members. "Why build museums when my family needs money for groceries?" one elder asked pointedly at a general council meeting. Others countered that long-term survival required investment in infrastructure, not just short-term distributions.

Leonard felt the weight of these debates personally. Every decision seemed to cut one way or another, creating factions that accused him of favoritism, selfishness or enslavement to special interests. He walked a narrow line. Too much generosity to individuals could hollow out the community's future. Too much emphasis on projects could fracture the fragile trust he had built.

Leonard's Resolve

Through it all, Leonard returned to his simple conviction that sovereignty meant making decisions for themselves as a collective entity, not letting outsiders dictate the terms. "We'll be judged either way," he told the council. "If we stay poor, they'll pity us. If we succeed, they'll resent us. But if we govern ourselves—if we decide our own path—then at least it's our path."

That conviction became his compass. Each time a headline questioned the tribe's wealth, or a legislator muttered about unfairness, Leonard reminded himself of the children in the day care, the elders in new homes, the students now attending college. These were not abstractions. They were lives transformed.

Still, he knew the battles ahead would not be fought only in bingo halls or community centers. They would play out in statehouses, courtrooms, and the halls of Congress. These were the places where sovereignty, once again, would be tested.

The Compacts of a Lifetime

The Spark at Lower Sioux

By the mid-1980s, Indian gaming had spread like a prairie fire across the country. High-stakes bingo halls were opening on reservations from Florida to California, and tribes were beginning to experiment with games that stretched beyond what states considered "charitable." Leonard Prescott, serving as chairman of the Shakopee Mdewakanton Sioux Community and as secretary–treasurer of the National Indian Gaming Association, kept one eye on Washington and the other on the developments closer to home.

One morning, while paging through the *Minneapolis StarTribune*, he read a story that made him stop cold. Just a hundred miles downriver, at the Lower Sioux Reservation where Leonard had lived as a boy, Jackpot Junction was now offering authentic Las Vegas-style blackjack—not the "bingo jack" variant Shakopee had used for years in its own bingo lounge, but the real game, with cards, dealers, and odds that looked exactly like the Vegas Strip.

The news traveled fast. Governor Arne Carlson called lobbyists to remind them that blackjack was not authorized in Minnesota's charitable gaming laws and had not been included in the 1990 compacts the state had signed with all eleven tribes. The state filed suit against Jackpot Junction, arguing the game was illegal.

Privately, Leonard thought his Lower Sioux relatives would lose in court. Publicly, he voiced support. Loyalty demanded nothing less. But he misjudged. When the dust settled, blackjack was declared permissible as an additional venue under charitable gaming. It was a shocking win—one that would ripple outward with consequences far larger than anyone in that courtroom realized.

Carlson himself, a cautious but pragmatic Republican, recognized that fighting blackjack through the courts could drag on for years, draining the state's coffers and yielding uncertain results. He was also wary of the hybrid games already offered in Tribal halls such as Bingo Jack and Bingo Roulette, the legality of which was already being stretched.

Carlson saw something else too—more jobs, increased revenues, and the possibility of tribes becoming genuine economic engines in Minnesota. Why fight an ambiguous case when the outcome could be *negotiated* instead? Why wage war when a compact could turn conflict into cooperation?

In conversations with Leonard, an idea emerged. Rather than continue the legal battle, the state could authorize a second round of compacts with the tribes that would add blackjack as a lawful game. It would be clean, efficient, and politically defensible.

Minnesota's Second Compacts

Leonard called a meeting of the Minnesota Indian Gaming Association. He relayed what Carlson and he had discussed. The discussion was brief but the logic was undeniable. The tribes endorsed the proposal for a second round of compacts unanimously.

To Leonard, the new blackjack compacts felt like more than a business deal. They carried the weight of history. *This is like the last treaty*, he thought—*an agreement between sovereigns, etched not in stone but in legal language that would prove surprisingly durable.*

The compacts predictably gave both sides the right to renegotiate terms in the future. But the key clause was stunning though subtle—neither party would be obligated to accept the other's proposed terms during renegotiation. If later negotiations failed, the original compact would remain intact. In practice, this meant the agreement could last indefinitely—functionally, it could exist *in perpetuity*.

Even more important, there were no stated caps. No limits on the number of blackjack tables in an enterprise. No ceilings on the number of video gaming machines. Expansion would be dictated by the tribes themselves according to their markets, not by state interference.

Another element, seldom recognized by the public, was tucked quietly into the Minnesota compacts—the tribes, not the state, would bear responsibility for the infrastructure and services needed to support their casinos. Unlike state-licensed racetracks or lotteries, which often relied on taxpayer-funded roads, utilities, and public safety services, the tribes agreed that they would finance their own.

This meant the Shakopee Mdewakanton Sioux Community and the other ten tribes would pay for water lines, sewer extensions, electricity, and road construction leading into their properties. They would also provide their own health care and social service facilities, including treatment for problem gambling or addiction, without asking the state to expand its own programs.

On the surface, this might have seemed like a lopsided deal favoring the state. Yet, for the tribes, it was a victory. It preserved the principle that the state could not disguise a tax by charging "impact fees" for utilities or health programs. By absorbing those costs themselves, the tribes kept both the revenues and the responsibilities under their own sovereign control.

This was a gift of regulatory freedom and recognition of Indian sovereignty that future generations of Tribal leaders would recognize as extraordinary. Leonard would later say this was part of why he considered the Minnesota agreements the "compact of a lifetime." They not only avoided revenue sharing but also ensured that tribes—not the state—decided how to reinvest in infrastructure, health care and their own People.

There was one more detail. It seemed small at the time, but in hindsight it proved colossal. The state insisted that it had to recoup the cost of auditing Tribal video games. In 1989, there were only six or seven hundred machines across all eleven tribes. The Charitable Gaming Commission estimated that oversight would cost about $10,000 per operation per year for state auditors to monitor compliance.

Leonard did the math. Using the current number of operations, this would total $150,000 annually for the entire state.

At the time, it seemed fair. Reasonable, even. But decades later, with Shakopee alone hosting over 4,500 machines and another 11,000 spread across Minnesota, the imbalance became glaring. A $4 billion industry was effectively regulated at a cost of pennies on the dollar.

To the public, Leonard knew this formula might look lopsided. To Leonard, however, it was sovereignty in practice. IGRA was clear—*states could not tax tribes*. What Minnesota and its tribes had agreed to in these compacts was not taxation, but a sovereign-to-sovereign business arrangement. Regulation had its place, but it would never become a Trojan horse for revenue extraction in Minnesota.

"Never Again" in Wisconsin and Beyond

Minnesota's compacts quickly became the envy of Indian Country—but also a target for state governments elsewhere. In Wisconsin, Governor Tommy Thompson took one look and vowed this kind of arrangement would never happen on his watch. He rejected the notion of open-ended compacts. Instead, he offered the tribes seven years, then reduced it to five, always ratcheting down the time horizon, always tightening the screws. He demanded payments to the state—call them taxes, call them gifts, call them "payments in lieu"—it made no difference. Without such payments, there would be no compacts.

In Leonard's eyes, Thompson's stance was extortion, plain and simple. Tribes on the cusp of economic liftoff found themselves halted at the door by the state's terms, forced to cut Wisconsin a piece of their future.

Elsewhere, it was even worse. In Connecticut, Foxwoods, the largest casino in the Western Hemisphere, which had opened at about the same time as Mystic Lake, agreed to hand over 25 percent of its revenues to the state, or $1 million annually, whichever was greater. This set a new precedent that lit a fire in governors' mansions across the country. If Connecticut could take a quarter of Tribal gaming dollars, why not New York, or California, or Arizona?

For Leonard, it was bitter to watch. *Never again*, he thought. Never again would Indian Country see the kind of respect Minnesota tribes had won.

The Long Shadow of Litigation

IGRA had provided one theoretical remedy for heavy-handed state terms. Tribes were allowed to sue states in federal court for failing to negotiate compacts in good faith. But lawsuits were slow, expensive, and subject to the political winds of the moment. A sympathetic Congress or Supreme Court could help, but hostile institutions could strip away sovereignty bit by bit.

Leonard knew the pattern well. Over the last eighty years, Tribal rights had risen and fallen with the tides of American politics.

Good years had brought recognition of sovereignty. Bad years had caused erosion of land, of rights, of power. States had always pressed to expand their reach. Tribes had always resisted.

Minnesota's blackjack compacts stood, for a time, as a rare exception—a glimpse of what true government-to-government relations might look like. But Leonard also knew the compacts were fragile, unique to their moment, unlikely ever to be repeated.

Beads for Manhattan

Looking back, Leonard could not resist an ironic comparison. In 1626, Dutch traders had purchased Manhattan from the Lenape for beads valued at $1,400. Three and a half centuries later, the tribes of Minnesota had signed compacts that gave them unlimited gaming potential in exchange for $150,000 per year in regulatory fees.

Who had made the better deal?

The answer was obvious to Leonard. The Minnesota compacts were not perfect, but they were the compacts of a lifetime. They gave his People a chance to stand on their own, to build housing, health care, and education, to show the state and the nation that sovereignty was not a relic of history but a living, breathing reality.

And he knew also that the window would not stay open forever.

The Backlash Begins

Word spread quickly that Minnesota's tribes had secured compacts with no revenue-sharing, no hard expiration dates, and no caps on machines or tables. To the tribes, it was a triumph of sovereignty. To many outside observers, though, it was heresy.

State legislators began receiving angry calls from constituents who asked why tribes were allowed to operate games while the state itself could not. Pastors warned from pulpits that casinos would bring addiction and ruin. Editorial boards of news organizations fretted about "special privileges" and wondered why Minnesota had "given away the store."

Leonard understood the subtext. For generations, Native People had been told, even by their own leaders, that they were incapable of managing land, money, or government. Now that tribes were building multi-million-dollar facilities and running them with efficiency, the narrative had shifted. It wasn't that Indians couldn't do it, it was that Indians *were not supposed to do it.*

The Shadow of Las Vegas

The loudest opposition came not from rural Minnesota but from far to the southwest. Las Vegas, already wary after Cabazon and IGRA, saw Minnesota's compacts as a threat to its dominance. If small tribes in the Upper Midwest could run casinos without state interference, what would stop tribes in Arizona, California or Wisconsin from doing the same?

Vegas casino lobbyists descended on Washington, warning senators of "unregulated casinos." They invoked the specter of organized crime, ignoring the fact that Tribal gaming operations were often more tightly monitored than private establishments. Behind the rhetoric was money—Las Vegas feared competition, and Minnesota had just set a precedent that could spread.

The Morality Front

Closer to home, churches framed the issue as one of morality. Gambling, they said, preyed on the poor and addicted. It did not matter that Minnesota already permitted charitable gaming through raffles, pull-tabs, and bingo nights in church basements. It did not matter that a state lottery had been launched with public fanfare. What mattered was that tribes were gaining independence through gaming. That independence unsettled old hierarchies.

Leonard listened to the sermons, read the editorials, and took note of the protests. He did not dismiss them. He had seen firsthand the damage alcohol and despair could cause. But he also knew that poverty was not morality. Poverty was captivity. And Mystic Lake, along with the blackjack compacts, was breaking chains that had shackled Native People for over a century.

Political Crosshairs

Acknowledging the growing opposition to Indian gaming and the compacts they had struck with the state, the Minnesota legislature convened hearings. Some lawmakers argued for tighter regulations, others for revenue-sharing. None could touch the compacts themselves—they were binding agreements. But the political theater was relentless.

Leonard found himself summoned to testify more than once. He walked the marble halls of the State Capitol in Saint Paul, facing panels of lawmakers who struggled to hide their resentment. "Why should your People be allowed to operate casinos tax-free?" one asked pointedly.

Leonard's answer was calm. "Because these are our lands, and we are sovereign governments. The United States recognized that when it signed treaties with our ancestors. This compact simply honors that principle."

This logic rooted in history was not always enough to silence critics, but it reminded them that Shakopee was not asking for favors—it was exercising rights.

A Sovereign Reality

As the controversy swirled, Mystic Lake thrived. Revenues climbed. Jobs multiplied. Housing and health care projects moved from plans on paper to bricks and mortar. For the first time in living memory, children of the Shakopee Mdewakanton Sioux Community looked forward to futures unshackled by scarcity.

The backlash could not erase that reality. Politicians could complain, churches could protest, and Las Vegas could lobby, but the compacts were signed. Minnesota's tribes had secured the space to build their own destinies.

For Leonard, the lesson was clear: Sovereignty was never granted freely. It had to be claimed, defended, and lived. The compacts were not the end of the battle, but they were proof that Native Nations could negotiate as equals—and win.

Lines of Blood and Lines of Power

Shortly after the historic gaming compacts were signed, the Shakopee Mdewakanton Sioux Community was engaged in a different, but equally consequential, negotiation—the reckoning with its own identity.

Gaming had changed everything. Once, the reservation lands were sparsely populated, economically barren, a place where only the most committed families clung to their inheritance. But by the end of the 1980s, the bingo hall, the video games of chance, and soon the blackjack tables had transformed Shakopee into something more than a curiosity. It was proof—living, breathing proof—that a Tribal community could seize sovereignty and make it profitable. And with that success came a flood of attention.

People across Indian Country began to see Shakopee as a beacon of possibility. Families who had once ignored or abandoned the land began to reconsider. Relatives who had long since drifted away, or whose lineage was questionable, suddenly saw an opportunity. Per capita payments derived from gaming revenues had replaced the old patchwork of state and federal funds, and the arguments over "who belonged" now carried *financial* weight.

The Enrollment Committee's Charge

In 1989, the Bureau of Indian Affairs instructed the SMSC enrollment committee to take stock. It was time to produce a list of qualified members under the constitutional criteria, a list that would determine not only political standing but also entitlement to the final judgment funds dating back to 1886.

That date was no accident. It tied directly to the aftermath of the US–Dakota War of 1862, when the federal government created special rolls for the "friendlies"—those Dakota families who had not participated in the uprising. Only descendants of the "friendlies," proven by documentary evidence, could claim rightful membership.

The work of the enrollment committee was painstaking. Its charge was not just to distribute benefits but to clarify identity—to draw the line between those who could legally and historically claim descent from the "friendlies" and those who could not. To make this case, the committee leaned on the testimony and memory of the elders, including one voice above all others—Leonard's mother, Rose Blossom Prescott.

Rose Blossom Prescott's Letter

In a letter to the Bureau of Indian Affairs in Washington, DC, Rose Prescott gave words to what the community had long felt but rarely documented. She wrote not as an administrator or politician, but as a woman who had lived the consequences of the government's neglect. Her letter, preserved in the archives, read in part:

> Since the establishment of these lands in 1886, the Bureau of Indian Affairs has failed in its fiduciary duty to keep track of the rightful heirs of the Mdewakanton who remained peaceful in the time of the uprising. These were the "friendlies," who did not take up arms

> and whose descendants were to inherit the use of these lands. Instead, over the years, people with no rightful claim were allowed to live here. Some were relatives by marriage, others were descendants of those who fought in 1862 and therefore excluded under the law. The Bureau's negligence has created confusion, anger, and hardship for those of us who can prove our lineage.
>
> We ask now that the government do what it should have done all along: recognize the rolls, recognize the bloodlines, and protect the rights of those whose ancestors who did not take part in the uprising. Without clarity, this community cannot survive as it was intended. The trust responsibility belongs not only to the Bureau, but to each generation that comes after. We are asking not for charity, but for recognition of what was promised.

The Stakes of Membership

Rose's words cut to the heart of the matter: The question of membership was not about favoritism or personal gain. It was about honoring a federal promise written into law in 1886 and ignored for generations.

The enrollment committee, armed with her testimony and with genealogical records, pressed forward. They enlisted the help of John Schade, who was then completing his training as a professional genealogist, to prepare the rolls. All purported members of the tribe were asked to submit an application for membership along with documentation supporting their blood degree and lineage to May 20, 1886.

The enrollment committee coordinated with local BIA agents and with Mitchell Bush, head of the Tribal Enrollment Program in Washington. Every safeguard was layered in, every effort made to ensure the process could withstand scrutiny. Some individuals claiming membership refused to submit their application or any documentation, which caused problems in subsequent elections in determining who was eligible to vote.

Still, the decisions carried pain. Families whose blood quantum fell just short of the one-quarter requirement found themselves excluded. Descendants of those who had participated in the uprising—however distant—were likewise disqualified. For those families, the exclusions felt arbitrary, even cruel. For others, the exclusions were the only way to safeguard the integrity of the community.

When the enrollment committee submitted its final list in 1991, the Bureau of Indian Affairs approved it and granted a three-month grace period for appeals. When that window closed, the Tribal roll was set. The community now had a definitive list of who belonged, and who did not.

Parallel Achievements, Parallel Strains

Even as the enrollment committee labored over bloodlines, the Tribal government was surging forward:

- Sewer and water agreements were negotiated with the city of Shakopee.
- The Tribal Court was established and Little Six was incorporated.
- Compacts were signed for video games of chance, then blackjack.
- Mystic Lake Casino was constructed.
- National leadership was gained through the National Indian Gaming Association.

- Statewide coordination was accomplished through the Minnesota Gaming Association.

Construction of Mystic Lake Casino on reservation land.
Little Six can be seen at the top.

Leonard Prescott, as chairman, worked closely with attorney Jim Townsend and Tribal Judge John Jacobson to craft compacts that gave SMSC the widest possible latitude. Yet, every advance demanded explanation, reassurance, and often personal persuasion. Leonard and his allies found themselves going house to house, family to family, convincing members that resolutions and ordinances were not just paperwork but the guardrails of survival.

The Political Storm

But prosperity did not bring peace. Every new success seemed to sharpen the old resentments. Families were still raw from the removal of Norm Crooks years earlier, and the Crooks family in particular viewed each Prescott achievement with suspicion and resentment.

The term for Tribal officers was nearing its end in 1991, and Leonard faced his greatest challenge yet—an election against Stan Crooks, heir to the grievances of his family and the standard-bearer for those who opposed the Prescott faction.

This was more than an election. It was a battle over memory and belonging, over who counted as a member and who held the right to lead. The compacts, the casino, the national leadership—all of it would be tested at the Mdewakanton ballot box in a contest where bloodlines and politics intertwined.

Looking back, Leonard understood that this election was the pivot point. Washington's negotiations had been difficult, Minnesota's compacts historic. But here, in Shakopee, the real battle began—not in marble corridors or legislative halls, but in living rooms, driveways, and community meetings where neighbors questioned one another's blood, loyalty, and legitimacy.

The storm of sovereignty was no longer just about gaming. It was about who belonged, and who would decide.

The Election of 1992

The BIA-approved Tribal roll specified who could vote in the upcoming election. The SMSC Constitution allowed for change in the Tribal roll, but only through a secretarial amendment requiring the approval of all BIA-recognized members. Such an amendment would demand near-impossible consensus in a community already fractured by family feuds and financial interests. One faction stood rigidly for the quarter-blood rule, another pressed to reduce the standard so their children and relatives could remain inside the circle.

Leonard Prescott, as chairman, felt the tension like a vise. He had walked into living rooms, sat at kitchen tables, and tried to persuade each family that compromise was the only path forward. Yet compromise meant touching blood itself, and for many, that was non-negotiable.

In private moments, Leonard leaned on his mother, Rose Blossom, and his sister, Pat. Both had served on the enrollment committee. Both carried a hard-won authority rooted in the memory of 1886 and the federal promise to the "friendlies." Their counsel was blunt—if Leonard ignored the federally-approved list and allowed non-qualified members to vote in the upcoming election, he would be no better than the leaders who had once opened the doors without criteria.

The Constitution itself was clear. If someone had been enrolled through fraud or error, the only remedy was to vote them out. The community had never exercised that clause, but the law remained. Rose and Pat told Leonard that the federal directive carried weight, and it was his duty to enforce it.

Leonard agreed. But agreeing with the principle did not erase the human pain. He thought often of the Welch family, who lived just across the way. Three or four of them had been admitted as members under Chairwoman Susan Totenhagen, had voted, and had received per capita checks. They had attended community meetings and lived as part of the fabric of Shakopee. Yet under the federal list, they fell just short—one thirty-second shy of the blood quantum required.

Leonard could not bring himself to blindside them on election day. He called the family together at the Tribal office. Sitting across from them, he explained that Washington had approved the rolls and that they had not made the cut. "It's not for lack of respect," he told them. "It's the law. And I cannot allow you to vote."

The room was tense. The Welches, good people and respected neighbors, listened. They told him plainly that they did not care much for either the Crooks or the Prescotts. But this was no longer about loyalty. It was about money, and they would vote for whomever best served their family's interest.

Leonard, trying to soften the blow, made them a promise. If reelected, his first act would be to draft an amendment to lower the blood standard so that families like theirs would not be cast out. The Welches nodded but gave no assurances.

As they left the meeting, Leonard's unease grew. He knew this election would be messy.

A Blizzard of Ballots

Election day came on November of 1992. The wind whipped snow across the prairie as Leonard sat in his mother's house, surrounded by sisters while waiting for the tally. He reminded himself of the work accomplished—compacts signed, Mystic Lake rising, ordinances and resolutions pushed through one living room conversation at a time. Surely, he thought, that record would carry the day.

But the storm outside mirrored the storm within.

When the votes were counted, Stan Crooks—son of Norman Crooks and the heir to the Crooks family's grievances—claimed victory. His supporters celebrated. Leonard's camp seethed. The objections came swiftly. The Prescotts, the Crooks, even the Welches raised challenges, arguing that ballots from disqualified or disputed members had been counted, tilting the result.

Into the Tribal Court

For the first time, the community turned to its newly established Tribal Court to settle the matter. The judges examined the record and found that some of the voters in question had participated in previous elections and meetings despite never being recognized by the enrollment committee. Did that long participation entitle them to a voice now? Or did the federal roll stand above custom?

After weeks of deliberation, the court took a cautious path. It placed the enrollment committee in abeyance until the disputes was resolved. With no active committee, no new determinations could be made.

But Stan Crooks would not wait. Declaring the court's pause intolerable, he convened his own meeting. Those he personally considered valid members—many of them without clear qualification under the Constitution—were assembled to form a "temporary" enrollment committee. That body immediately began processing applications, opening the door to new memberships with little or no legal foundation.

Then Stan went further. He bypassed the unresolved Tribal Court, went directly to the Bureau of Indian Affairs with the election results, and persuaded that body to recognize his chairmanship. The BIA, either unaware of the disputes or unwilling to wade into them, validated the outcome.

A Heartbroken Reckoning

For Leonard and his family, the blow was crushing. Years of work—carefully crafted rolls, federal verification, and the hard discipline of saying no to neighbors—were suddenly swept aside. The standards of 1886, the quarter-blood requirement, the principle of integrity in membership—all these things seemed in danger of being erased.

In its place, Leonard saw the specter of what he had most feared—a free-for-all, where membership was determined not by history or law, but by faction and finance. With gaming dollars now flowing, membership itself had become a prize, and it was now open to manipulation.

The irony was bitter. Leonard had carried the tribe to national recognition, had stood shoulder to shoulder with senators and governors, had fought to defend sovereignty in Washington. Yet at home, in the small circle of families that made up the SMSC, sovereignty was unraveling from within.

The Crooks Ascendancy

Scorched Earth

Stan Crooks' chairmanship began not with reconciliation or vision, but with destruction. His first mission, carried out within hours of being recognized by the Bureau of Indian Affairs, was to dismantle the record of work achieved by the enrollment committee over the prior three years.

The day after the BIA validated his election, Stan and his newly formed business council—many of them unqualified under the Constitution—marched into the enrollment office. Filing cabinets were emptied, documents shredded, genealogies discarded. Three years of meticulous research, correspondence with Washington, and verification of 1886 descent were annihilated in a single sweep. It was a symbolic act as much as a practical one: the erasure of history that had threatened the Crooks family's claims to legitimacy.

For Leonard Prescott and others who had labored to establish a credible roll, it was devastating. The SMSC's one chance to fix its membership, to align law with lineage, had been thrown away. Sovereignty, which Leonard had defended so fiercely in Washington and St. Paul, was rendered meaningless at home, drowned in factional ambition.

Stanley Crooks.

Inheritance and Contradiction

Stan's reign immediately lapsed into turmoil. General council meetings devolved into shouting matches, even fistfights. M-14 rifles were fired by one faction, returned in kind by another. Trust was shattered, fear commonplace.

Yet, alongside that chaos was astonishing prosperity. When Leonard took office in 1985, the community's economy stood at $16 million. By the time Stan seized power, the SMSC economy had grown to nearly $500 million dollars—$496 million by conservative measure. Mystic Lake, the compacts, Little Six, Inc., the Tribal court, charitable giving, and the respect of national politicians and lawyers—all of it lay within Stan's grasp.

It was, paradoxically, both the best and worst moment to inherit the chairmanship. The government was divided and raw, but the coffers were full.

The Membership Question

For Stan, the most urgent problem was not governance or economic growth. It was membership. The Crooks family, like others aligned with them, did not meet the constitutional standards required for per capita distribution. Under the SMSC Constitution and the Indian Gaming Regulatory Act, members had to be at least one-quarter Mdewakanton Sioux and trace descent to the 1886 "friendlies." Without that proof, they should have been excluded.

Stan's solution was blunt. He fired the legal counsel who had defended the community's positions in Congress and in court. He hired new lawyers, handpicked to defend his own policies, no matter how inconsistent with the Constitution. Then he set about constructing a system by which non-qualified individuals could be admitted and existing loyalties rewarded.

Some relatives were simply granted membership without application, their names added to rolls by virtue of kinship. Others were promised per capita payments set aside in special accounts. These individuals were assured that once "adoption ordinances" were approved, their benefits would be restored. It was membership not by descent, but by convenience and allegiance.

The truly qualified members, who had endured years of genealogical research and federal scrutiny, saw what was happening. They protested to the BIA's local area director, Earl Barlow, who agreed that the adoption ordinances conflicted with the Constitution and initially disapproved them. Washington itself sent confirmation that membership criteria could only be changed through a secretarial election, not by fiat.

But Stan was undeterred. He had the votes he needed—many from individuals without verifiable ties to 1886—and he had no intention of letting constitutional language block his path.

History and Its Manipulation

The irony was stark. The 1886 lands had been set aside specifically for the "friendlies," those Mdewakantons who had refused to join the uprising of 1862, often at great personal risk. Their descendants—Leonard's family among them—had spent a century guarding those fragile rights, despite poverty and neglect.

Stan's family history was different. Norman Crooks, Stan's father, had remained enrolled with the Santee Sioux Tribe of Nebraska as late as 1975. Under the SMSC Constitution, no person enrolled in another tribe could also claim Shakopee membership. The rule was not arbitrary—the 1886 trust lands were designated for homeless Indians who had severed their ties elsewhere in order to remain in Minnesota.

For the Crooks' descendants, this presented a dilemma. Their bloodlines did not qualify them under the quarter-blood standard, nor did their family history tie them to the 1886 rolls. To remain in power, they needed to rewrite the narrative by substituting respect for figures like Chief Little Crow, Wabasha, and Medicine Bottle as symbolic elders, while ignoring the legal and historical distinctions that set the "friendlies" apart.

Leonard saw it for what it was—a masquerade of false history. "If you don't know if a member is qualified," he asked, "how do you know if a Tribal leader is qualified? And if that's true, how does the federal government know if it is truly dealing on a government-to-government basis?"

The Consequences of Power

Stan wasted no time consolidating authority. He purged Mystic Lake's leadership, firing eighteen top personnel—the CEO, presidents and vice-presidents of blackjack and video games, the head of personnel, and Leonard himself, who had been serving as chairman of the board of directors. He dismissed the sovereign corporate structures that Leonard's administration had carefully built even as he wielded their powers to direct millions in charitable gifts wherever he wished. Every decision, large or small, now required Stan's approval.

The proverb proved apt—*power corrupts, and absolute power corrupts absolutely*. Stan had inherited the money, the buildings, the staff, the guards, and the stature. But instead of stewarding them for the community's long-term stability, he used them to fortify his own position and entrench non-qualified members at the heart of government.

The Larger Failure

To Leonard, the tragedy was not Stan's doing alone. It was the federal government's abdication of its fiduciary duty. Treaties had long been ignored or twisted. Constitutions were treated as malleable suggestions, left to the interpretation of whoever happened to hold office. When the community was poor—living on dirt roads in inadequate housing—Washington looked the other way. Now that the SMSC was wealthy beyond precedent, the absence of oversight turned into an invitation for abuse.

The result was two classes of membership—those who had proved their descent from the 1886 rolls and those who had not. The first group carried the burden of history and verification; the second, the convenience of political favor.

That, Leonard believed, was the crux of Shakopee's troubles. "Where you find a lot of money," he reflected, "you will also find people trying to get at it for themselves."

National Reverberations

What happened inside Shakopee did not stay there. News of Stan's maneuvering spread quickly through the tight network of Tribal leaders, lobbyists, and congressional aides who tracked Indian gaming developments.

For outsiders, it confirmed their worst suspicions. Governors already wary of the Minnesota compacts pointed to Shakopee as proof that tribes, left to themselves, could not maintain internal order. "Look," they would say, "at the factional disputes, the questionable membership rolls, the family feuds masquerading as government." Legislators in Washington seized upon these stories to argue that federal oversight should be tightened, that sovereignty could not mean carte blanche.

The irony was bitter. Leonard's administration had worked to prove that sovereignty could be exercised responsibly—that tribes could negotiate compacts as equals, manage casinos with professionalism, and use revenues to build community institutions. Stan inherited that record but then distorted the perception. His manipulation of membership rolls, his purging of professional staff, and his consolidation of authority fed a narrative that tribes were not ready for unrestrained self-determination.

In the states, governors began to demand more from compact negotiations. Wisconsin's Tommy Thompson pointed to Shakopee's chaos when justifying higher payments to the state. Connecticut, facing the explosive growth of Foxwoods, used Shakopee as an example when insisting on a staggering 25 percent share of Tribal gaming revenues. What Minnesota had secured—a sovereign-to-sovereign compact that placed no limits on machines and virtually no expiration—would never be repeated. Other tribes would pay the price.

Sovereignty on Trial

Even within Indian Country, the consequences were unsettling. Tribes who had fought hard to prove their legitimacy to Congress now found themselves explaining why Shakopee's internal disputes should not taint them all. Membership, the sacred question of belonging, was now viewed by outsiders as a tool to manipulate access to gaming dollars.

For Leonard, the frustration was acute. He saw how national allies—men like Senator Inouye and Representative George Miller—had to spend political capital defending Tribal sovereignty against critics who pointed to Shakopee. Sovereignty itself, he feared, was being put on trial not because of hostile state governments, but because of decisions made by Tribal leaders who placed self-interest above constitutional integrity.

The Paradox of Success

The paradox was unmistakable. The very success that had lifted Shakopee out of poverty now gave ammunition to those who wanted to limit sovereignty nationwide. The $700 million casino, the charitable gifts, the headlines about per capita payments—all this became evidence in debates over whether Indian gaming had gone "too far."

The completed Mystic Lake Casino in 1992.

And yet, Leonard knew, the real story was more complicated. Shakopee had proven what was possible when sovereignty was honored. In just a few years, a community that had once been dismissed as marginal had become an economic powerhouse. Roads were paved, housing was built, health care improved, and a generation of children grew up with opportunities their parents had never dreamed of.

But the abuse of that power—altering membership rolls, silencing dissent, concentrating authority in a single family—threatened to erase the gains by undermining the moral foundation on which sovereignty rested.

The Dismantling of Little Six

The story of Little Six, Inc.—its creation, its promise, and its destruction—is not simply about corporate structure. It is about whether sovereignty could be exercised with integrity, and whether a community that had clawed its way out of poverty would defend institutions built to protect it from politics and factionalism.

Building a Firewall Between Politics and Business

During Leonard Prescott's administration, Shakopee sought to separate business from government. Everyone knew what could happen if family disputes and political rivalries were allowed to intrude into casino operations—chaos, favoritism, and self-dealing. To prevent that, the tribe retained the highly regarded Lindquist & Vennum law firm to draft a business ordinance and charter a Tribally-owned corporation—Little Six, Inc.—to manage all commercial enterprises, including gaming, hospitality, and entertainment.

A board of directors, elected by the general council, had been established. The ordinance itself was written to withstand the storms of politics. Any change to Little Six's structure or authority would require a two-thirds vote of the membership—and then, in a safeguard almost unheard of, a second two-thirds vote would be needed to confirm that decision. It was, in effect, a firewall against the short-term impulses of politics.

The principle was simple. The general council would oversee social services and governmental functions; the corporation would manage business. And for the first time in the community's history, members became shareholders, each person bound not by rumor and faction but by the responsibilities of a corporate structure.

This was a radical experiment. Many members balked. They wanted management jobs in the new operations, positions they believed they deserved by birthright. "What do you think we are, stupid Indians?" some said. Others accused the leadership of stealing their rights. But Leonard had stood firm. "We cannot grow," he argued, "if our businesses are run like family fiefdoms."

Little Six on the Rise

Under Leonard's firm hand, the early years proved the wisdom of that decision. Little Six, Inc. quickly expanded beyond gaming. Within three years, it launched Mahto Industries—"Mahto" meaning "bear" in Dakota—after acquiring a struggling equipment manufacturer in Oakes, North Dakota. The town celebrated the purchase with a parade, hailing Shakopee as a savior for its largest employer.

Another venture, Windot, was formed in partnership with Minnesota's Fortune 500 giant 3M. It manufactured recyclable bingo paper, piloted with tribes in Michigan, Oklahoma, and California, and stood ready for national expansion.

Awards followed. Mystic Lake Casino and its sister property, Little Six, were recognized for performance and innovation. Revenues climbed. The corporate model worked.

Jealousies and the Seeds of Dismantling

Success, however, can breed jealousy. When Stan Crooks assumed the chairmanship, he inherited an economy that had grown from $16 million in 1985 to nearly $500 million by 1992, supported by strong management and corporate diversification. But instead of embracing the model, Stan and his allies saw in it a threat to their control.

Soon, a small outside accounting firm was retained at the recommendation of the Blue Dog law firm, aided by Faegre & Benson. Their task was to pierce the corporate protection surrounding Little Six. Allegations followed—misrepresentation, misapplication of funds, accusations conjured more from suspicion than fact.

The gaming commission, headed by Stan's daughter, seized upon these charges. Leonard was removed as chairman and CEO of Little Six. Alongside him, President and COO Bill Johnson was dismissed from the Board.

The maneuver sent shockwaves throughout the operation. Key employees—many who had built Mystic Lake from the ground up—resigned. Mahto Industries faltered. Windot collapsed. What had been carefully insulated from politics was pulled back under Tribal government control where it could be bent to factional will.

Years of Litigation

The charges against Leonard and Johnson did not stand. After years of legal wrangling, a Tribal court dismissed them via summary judgment. But the damage was done. Leonard's effectiveness as a leader was undermined, and his personal finances were drained in defending himself. Unlike Stan, who used Tribal resources to cover his legal costs, Leonard bore his expenses personally.

Even when acquitted, the pursuit did not end. Stan launched new lawsuits, seizing upon an indemnification clause in corporate law meant to protect employees falsely accused of crimes. Payments authorized under that clause were recast as evidence of misconduct. This unnecessary and expensive litigation stretched on for seventeen years. Ultimately, Leonard was ordered to pay back $1.7 million to the community he had once led despite the clear intent of national Indian gaming law that casino revenues not be used in such ways.

The reach of the campaign went beyond Tribal court. Stan's vengeful administration pressed state courts, sought reversals, and even petitioned federal courts to ensure Leonard could not escape liability. Judges questioned conflicts of interest—Tribal attorney Steve Olsen, for example, represented nearly every arm of the government simultaneously—but the pressure wore on. Federal courts repeatedly sent cases back, entangling Leonard in an exhausting cycle of appeals.

Erasing a Legacy

Perhaps the deepest wound was not financial but historical. When the Shakopee Mdewakanton Cultural Center was built, its timeline of community history omitted the years of Leonard's administration almost entirely. The remade record leaped from 1969, mentioning Norman Crooks, to 1992, when Stan assumed power. The years between—the years of compacts, corporate structuring, diversification, and unprecedented growth—were collapsed into a footnote.

Leonard could only watch as the adoptees and their allies reinterpreted history, plucking away feather by feather the contributions of those who had built the foundation. He recalled Madeleine Albright's observation about Mussolini: "If you pluck a chicken one feather at a time, no one will ever notice."

A Sobering Question

In the end, Little Six, Inc. was dismantled not because it failed, but because it succeeded. It proved that Shakopee could govern its businesses with professionalism, that Tribal sovereignty could produce innovation and prosperity. But it also proved vulnerable to the oldest dangers of envy, factionalism, and the hunger for control.

Leonard was left to ask a sobering question. Were they building a society to be proud of, one grounded in law, history, and shared prosperity? Or had power become a tyranny, overshadowing the very survival and resilience that had once defined the community?

The Corporate Consequences

The immediate consequence of dismantling Little Six, Inc. was the collapse of diversification. The subsidiary companies—Mahto Industries in North Dakota and the Windot joint venture with 3M—had been bold attempts to prove that Tribal gaming revenue could seed sustainable, non-gaming enterprises. For the first time in generations, the SMSC had been seen not simply as a poor reservation in Minnesota but as a player in national business circles. The parade in Oaks, North Dakota, celebrating Mahto Industries was more than civic theater; it was the symbol of a town's lifeline being preserved by Indian capital.

All of that had now come apart. Once Stan Crooks' administration moved against Little Six's leadership, investors backed away. The fragile trust that had been built with outside partners dissolved in the heat of Tribal politics. Mahto closed. Windot faded. Watching closely, potential partners in other states saw risk instead of reliability.

Inside Shakopee, the dismantling reinforced the message that political loyalty outweighed professional competence. The resignations of Bill Johnson and other senior staff gutted institutional memory. Employees who had built Mystic Lake from the ground up—through trial, error, and innovation—were shown the door. The new order made it clear that success mattered less than control.

A Shift in Governance

The dissolution of Little Six also marked a philosophical shift. Under Leonard Prescott's administration, business had been placed behind a firewall—a Tribally chartered corporation with bylaws, boards, and protections against the chimera of politics. Once that firewall was breached, the general council again held direct sway over the day-to-day affairs of multimillion-dollar enterprises with predictable consequences.

What had been envisioned as a sovereign experiment in corporate law reverted to the older pattern of government-as-business, where per capita payments, hiring, and contracts were filtered through family ties and factional alliances. The distinction between *citizen* and *shareholder*, so carefully crafted, quickly evaporated.

This shift reverberated well beyond Shakopee. Other tribes, considering whether to adopt similar corporate structures, now faced second thoughts. "If they couldn't protect Little Six," one Tribal lawyer in Wisconsin remarked at the time, "what chance do we have against our own factions?"

The Historical Consequences

In hindsight, Little Six, Inc. represented a moment when Indian Country stood on the cusp of redefining itself. For decades, the standard critique from outsiders had been that tribes could not run their own economies without federal supervision. Little Six's existence directly contradicted that stereotype. It showed that tribes could adopt sophisticated corporate models, diversify, and even engage with Fortune 500 companies on equal footing.

The dismantling of Little Six, therefore, was not just the fall of a corporation—it was the loss of a demonstration project for sovereignty itself. Where there might have been decades of precedent proving the viability of Tribal corporate charters insulated from politics, there was instead a cautionary tale.

Academics and legal scholars picked up on it. Case studies that once praised Shakopee's innovation turned into laments about missed opportunities. Conferences that had once cited Mystic Lake as the frontier of Tribal capitalism now warned of the dangers of internal collapse.

National Implications

At the national level, the timing could not have been worse. The 1990s were a decade of explosive growth in Indian gaming, and with that growth came backlash. States pushed for more power. Governors, legislators, and state gaming commissions looked for evidence that tribes were mismanaging their enterprises, that sovereignty was a loophole for chaos. Shakopee's turmoil gave them exactly that.

The dismantling of Little Six became an anecdote wielded in congressional hearings. "Even Shakopee," critics would say, "the richest little tribe in America, couldn't keep their corporate house in order." This line was repeated by lobbyists representing state governments, charitable gaming associations, and Las Vegas interests.

The blow was not only external. Within the National Indian Gaming Association (NIGA), Shakopee's loss of institutional credibility weakened its voice. Leonard Prescott, once chairman of NIGA, had been forced to spend years defending himself in Tribal and state courts. His absence helped create a vacuum in national leadership. Other tribes stepped in, but the example Shakopee had once provided—that a tiny community could lead by professionalism—was gone.

A Broader Lesson

The dismantling of Little Six reminded Indian Country of a painful truth—sovereignty is only as strong as the structures built to sustain it. Charters, ordinances, and corporate shields are words on paper unless a community is prepared to defend them against the temptations of factional gain.

In that sense, the fall of Little Six became part of a larger national story. Across Indian Country, tribes struggled with the same dilemma—how to manage sudden wealth without repeating the mistakes of past centuries when divisions had left Native Nations vulnerable to outside pressure. Shakopee's experience was a stark lesson that internal fracture could be as dangerous as external enemies.

Weaponized Narratives: Wisconsin

The Wisconsin example, mentioned earlier, was immediate. Governor Tommy Thompson, already wary of the Minnesota compacts, seized on Shakopee's internal disputes as evidence that tribes could not be trusted to regulate themselves.

In negotiations with Wisconsin tribes, Thompson's team referenced Shakopee explicitly. "Look at Minnesota," they would say. "Even the Shakopee Sioux, with all their money, can't control their own gaming board. Factions fire managers, destroy records, sue each other in court. And you expect us to hand over regulatory authority?"

The result was a set of compacts far weaker than Minnesota's. Where Minnesota tribes had secured agreements with no tax or revenue-sharing requirements, Wisconsin tribes were forced into seven-year compacts, subject to renewal, and pressured to accept "payments in lieu of taxes." Thompson openly declared, "I don't care what you call it—it's going to the state."

Behind the rhetoric was a strategy—use Shakopee's disarray to argue that Tribal sovereignty was impractical. If Shakopee could not maintain a corporate structure, then Wisconsin would "protect" its tribes by imposing tighter state controls.

The irony was sharp. The dismantling of Little Six had been an internal political maneuver, not a failure of corporate law. But Thompson and his allies blurred that distinction. They told the public that Tribal gaming needed state oversight because even the "richest Indian tribe in America" could not govern itself without scandal.

Weaponized Narratives—Connecticut

Connecticut went further. The rise of the Mashantucket Pequot's Foxwoods Casino and the Mohegan Sun created immense political pressure. State legislators, fearing the scale of Tribal gaming revenues, used Shakopee as Exhibit A in arguments for revenue sharing.

"If Minnesota's tribes can fall into chaos," Connecticut lobbyists argued, "then surely we need guarantees that revenues are managed responsibly. The state must have its share."

That logic became the justification for Connecticut's infamous compact requiring the Pequots to pay 25 percent of their slot revenue—or a minimum of $1 million a year, whichever was greater—to the state. This compact, hailed at the time as a model, was in reality a precedent for legalized extortion.

The argument rested, in part, on Shakopee. Shakopee's internal strife was pointed to as proof that Tribal governments could not be trusted with unchecked revenues. Better, the state said, to skim off a portion "for the public good."

The Domino Effect

From there, the weaponization spread. Legislators in New Mexico, South Dakota, and Wyoming cited Shakopee's internal lawsuits as cautionary tales. Editorials in regional newspapers referenced "the Shakopee mess" as evidence that tribes needed tighter state controls.

This was the national consequence—a narrative of dysfunction that undermined sovereignty. What had begun as an internal fight over Little Six became ammunition for governors and lobbyists across the country.

What Was Lost

The damage was not only financial. What was lost was the chance for Shakopee to serve as a model of Tribal professionalism. Had Little Six survived intact, it could have stood as a shield for other tribes facing hostile governors. Instead, its collapse became a cudgel.

Minnesota remained exceptional because of its early compacts, but elsewhere the pattern was grim—short-term agreements, heavy revenue sharing, and states emboldened to treat sovereignty as negotiable.

Shakopee's struggle, in other words, became everyone's struggle.

NIGA on the Defensive

For the National Indian Gaming Association, this was a crisis. NIGA had been founded to protect sovereignty, to show Congress that tribes were capable of regulating themselves responsibly. Now, Shakopee's story was being retold as a parable of corruption and chaos.

At strategy sessions, NIGA leaders debated their response. Some argued that Shakopee should be defended outright, that every Tribal government had the right to resolve internal disputes in its own way. Others, more pragmatic, insisted that NIGA had to distance itself from Shakopee's politics or risk losing credibility with Congress.

Leonard remembered the shift vividly. Where once Shakopee had been praised as a pioneer—bringing video gaming to the table, pushing for strong compacts—now lobbyists warned him quietly in

Washington corridors: "Keep your head down. Shakopee is toxic in DC right now."

The Capitol Hill Calculus

On Capitol Hill, NIGA's message became sharper. Leaders such as Billie Houle, Joel Frank, and Buzz Gutierrez stressed that Indian Country was not a monolith. Yes, Shakopee was in turmoil, but that turmoil did not define the national movement.

NIGA's testimony before the Senate Select Committee on Indian Affairs began to include carefully crafted talking points:

- Tribal gaming was already among the most tightly regulated industries in the country, subject to three layers of oversight—Tribal, federal, and, in many cases, state.
- Instances of internal conflict did not invalidate sovereignty any more than corruption in state governments invalidated statehood.
- The story of Indian gaming was one of success—jobs created, schools funded, hospitals built—not of scandal.

But behind closed doors, NIGA knew it had to double its efforts. Lobbyists were dispatched to reassure wary lawmakers. Funds were raised to commission economic impact studies. A quiet but deliberate effort was launched to shift the narrative away from Shakopee and back to the national picture of Tribal self-sufficiency.

Leonard's Personal Role

For Leonard, this was a bitter turn. He had been among the earliest officers of NIGA, serving as secretary–treasurer during its fragile beginnings. Now, he found himself sidelined, his community's troubles weaponized against the very movement he had helped build.

Still, he spoke where he could. At one gathering, Leonard reminded his peers, "We are not here to be perfect in the eyes of Congress. We are here to be sovereign in the eyes of our People. Mistakes will be made. But sovereignty means we have the right to make them, and the right to correct them."

It was a defiant truth, but in Washington, nuance rarely carried the day. Headlines were simpler: "Shakopee in Turmoil" and "Tribal Casino Infighting Raises Questions."

The Broader Consequence

In the end, NIGA managed to hold the line. Congress did not use Shakopee as the trigger for rolling back the Indian Gaming Regulatory Act (IGRA). But the damage lingered. Governors like Tommy Thompson in Wisconsin and officials in Connecticut found it easier to demand revenue-sharing concessions by pointing to Shakopee as an example of "why tribes needed supervision."

The irony was that Shakopee's early innovations—the very breakthroughs that had given Indian Country a foothold in gaming—were now being rewritten as cautionary tales.

For NIGA, the lesson was sobering: One tribe's internal politics could ripple across the continent, reshaping negotiations in states thousands of miles away.

The Battle Over Adoptees

From the very beginning of his chairmanship, Stan Crooks set his sights on membership. If money was the bloodstream of sovereignty, then membership rolls were its heart, and Stan understood that control of those rolls meant control of the entire body. His method was simple—adoption ordinances.

He presented these ordinances as legal pathways to full membership, assuring families that adoption would open the doors to per capita payments and other benefits. The truth was otherwise. Under the SMSC Constitution, the word *adoption* had never meant the wholesale addition of people without the required criteria. It had meant adopting a *process*—integrating qualified descendants who met the standards of 1886 ancestry and one-quarter blood. Stan's move, however, was something else entirely—a redefinition of identity itself.

A Precedent Misused

In the entire history of the community, only two adoptees had ever been recognized. One was Leonard's mother, Rose Blossom Prescott. Her adoption came under extraordinary circumstances, during the administration of Stan's father, Norman Crooks. Rose was granted eligibility for Tribal benefits but not for federal programs. Her case was one of compassion, not politics, and it was acknowledged that she lacked the 1886 lineal descent required for full qualification.

The other adoptee was Ario Haase, who had given much to the cultural life of the tribe. He was made an honorary member, without eligibility for per capita distributions. His adoption was symbolic, a recognition of contribution rather than an opening of the treasury.

Stan's ordinances inverted this precedent. Instead of exceptional cases, he sought to make adoption the rule—and to tie it directly to money and power.

The First Ordinance

The first adoption ordinance, Ordinance No. 10-27-93-001, exposed the raw tactics at play. In its first vote, the general council rejected the ordinance by a single ballot, 31–30. Then, after most members had left, those remaining called for a second vote. This time it passed 30–0.

It was a maneuver so brazen it seemed almost farcical, but the implications were grave. The Bureau of Indian Affairs, through Acting Area Director Carol Bacon, quickly disapproved the ordinance. Her November 12, 1993 letter cut to the core:

> The Adoption Ordinance would establish a fourth category of members... The net effect... is to eliminate the 1/4 blood requirement from the second category, which I do not believe can or should be accomplished by other than an Amendment to the Constitution... The ordinance, if approved, would automatically enroll 165 individuals... more than doubling the community's population.

The verdict was unmistakable—adoption ordinances could not replace constitutional amendments.

The Second Ordinance

Undeterred, Stan tried again. Ordinance No. 11-30-93-002 promised to address the BIA's concerns, but in substance it was the same. Acting Area Director Vincent Keslua's December 13, 1993 letter was equally blunt:

> The Adoption Ordinance circumvents the Constitution by attempting to accomplish by Ordinance what the Community's Constitution requires to be done by Constitutional Amendment… It would affect the very fabric of the Community.

Yet, despite another disapproval, Stan treated the ordinance as though it had passed. He returned withheld per capita payments to the adoptees and permitted them to draw full benefits. Thirty new members were added to a roll that had previously counted just seventy-eight. None of them met constitutional criteria.

Stan then appealed to Washington. The BIA's Central Office initially upheld the local disapproval. But months later, the Interior Board of Indian Appeals reversed course. While acknowledging that both the Area Office and the community had reasonable interpretations of the Constitution, the IBIA deferred to "Tribal sovereignty" and allowed the community's reading to stand.

A Constitutional Amendment Attempt

Under mounting scrutiny, Stan eventually conceded that only a constitutional amendment could settle the question. A secretarial election was called. But in a bitter irony, the newly adopted members—whose eligibility was precisely the issue at stake—were allowed to vote.

Ada Deer, then assistant secretary for Indian affairs, intervened. On June 2, 1995, she denied the amendment, citing voting irregularities and affirming the sanctity of constitutional processes. It was a rare and forceful assertion of federal trust responsibility.

In the election for Tribal chair in early 1996, however, Stan Crooks again triumphed over Leonard Prescott, chiefly due to the allowance of ineligible votes for Crooks. Out of 105 ballots, forty-six were cast by people not qualified to vote by both the community's own constitution and by the written determinations of the BIA in 1991. Nearly 90 percent of the ineligible voters had been illegally adopted as "members" during Stan Crooks' first term. If these ineligible ballots had been thrown out, Prescott would have won by six votes.

The Third Ordinance

After winning another term as chair, Stan pressed forward. In 1997, a third adoption ordinance was drafted—Resolution No. 05-13-97-002. By now, federal fatigue and political lobbying tilted the balance. The ordinance was tacitly approved when Assistant Secretary Kevin Gover declined to act within the ninety-day window. The inaction carried the force of approval.

Gover's resignation came shortly afterward, and his subsequent employment with Steptoe & Johnson—a law firm retained by Stan Crooks' administration—only deepened suspicions. Tribal members watched as lobbyists and attorneys seemed to shape decisions once reserved for constitutional authority.

The National Stakes

For Leonard, the adoptee battle was never just about Shakopee. He traveled to Washington, carried boxes of documents, and argued that if constitutions could be bent so easily, then sovereignty itself was at risk. "A government must first identify who they are," he insisted, "before they can ask others to respect them."

What had once been a matter of ancestry and legal criteria was now a political commodity. Gaming revenues made membership worth more than gold. In the past, with poor housing and dirt roads, few outsiders clamored for enrollment. After Mystic Lake, enrollment rolls became battlegrounds.

The adoptee ordinances were the hinge. They blurred the line between qualified and unqualified, between constitutional right and political favor. And in doing so, they gave ammunition to critics across Indian Country who argued that tribes lacked the discipline to govern membership fairly.

National Consequences

The adoptee ordinances did not remain a private quarrel inside the walls of the Community Center in Shakopee. Word traveled quickly. Lobbyists in Saint Paul carried whispers to Washington. Attorneys working for states in compact negotiations pointed to Shakopee's turmoil as Exhibit A for why tribes could not be trusted with unfettered sovereignty.

What had once been a local fight over family names and blood quantum became a national talking point. The question was simple but devastating. If a tribe could, by ordinance, adopt dozens—or hundreds—of new members without constitutional authority, what stopped them from expanding indefinitely, creating citizens out of thin air and distributing casino revenues to anyone they chose?

In state capitols and on Capitol Hill, opponents of Indian gaming seized on the example. Governors who had already bristled at the notion of compacts in perpetuity now found rhetorical fuel. "Look at Shakopee," they would say. "If tribes can invent members, then they can invent voters, invent beneficiaries, and evade accountability."

The Connecticut and Wisconsin Echoes

The timing was unfortunate. In Connecticut, Foxwoods had exploded onto the scene, quickly becoming the largest casino in the Western Hemisphere. The state, however, demanded 25 percent of slot revenues, an arrangement tribes accepted under pressure. Shakopee's membership controversies were quietly referenced in those negotiations: Why not demand a cut if tribes were already bending their own rules to enlarge the pie?

In Wisconsin, Governor Tommy Thompson flatly rejected Minnesota's model of government-to-government compacts without taxation. He demanded payments, no matter what name was given them. Behind closed doors, aides pointed to Shakopee's adoptee disputes as justification: If membership rolls could be manipulated for money, then surely the state had a right to claim its share.

The View from Washington

Inside the National Indian Gaming Association, the adoptee issue became a headache. Leonard remembered long strategy sessions where allies from California, Florida, and the Dakotas tried to hold a unified line—sovereignty first, compacting second. But reporters and congressional staffers kept circling back to Shakopee. "Isn't your own tribe expanding membership just to increase payouts?" they would ask.

The danger was existential. If tribes could not demonstrate discipline in their own governance, Congress might seize the opening to rewrite IGRA, tightening federal control over enrollment, per capita payments, and compact negotiations. For NIGA, it became critical to separate the larger national movement from Shakopee's internal disputes.

A Wound That Would Not Heal

For Leonard, the sting was personal. He had spent years defending sovereignty in Washington, warning that states and Congress were always looking for excuses to chip away at treaty rights. Now, his own community, under Stan's ordinances, had handed them ammunition.

He carried boxes of documents—BIA disapprovals, Department of the Interior letters, enrollment records—to congressional offices and law schools, insisting that Shakopee's Constitution still mattered. "We are not a country club," he would say. "We are a nation, and our membership rolls are as sacred as any nation's citizenship."

But the damage was done. Shakopee's adoptee battles became part of the national story of Indian gaming—an example cited by critics, a caution whispered by allies, and a shadow over every negotiation that followed.

Into the Courts

After the Interior Board of Indian Appeals allowed Shakopee's Adoption Ordinance II to stand, the matter spilled into federal courtrooms. A small group of quarter-blood members, armed with genealogical records and the Constitution itself, argued that the ordinances violated the most basic promise of self-government—that membership was to be grounded in the 1886 rolls and the quarter-blood requirement.

Judge Robinson, presiding, pressed the Department of the Interior with pointed questions. Why had the Bureau exceeded its ninety-day review period by nearly a year? Did the BIA ever investigate whether ineligible individuals had voted in the first place? And what authority, exactly, did Chairman Stan Crooks have to pursue appeals without a resolution from the general council?

The Department's answers were halting. They admitted the ninety-day deadline had lapsed. They admitted they had not investigated the disputed votes. Yet the IBIA's ruling remained, and adoption ordinances—now twice rejected by local BIA offices—were still tacitly alive in Washington.

For Leonard, it was a Kafkaesque cycle. The federal government, which had insisted for generations that Indian identity must be proven through census rolls and blood quantum, was now shrugging off violations of those very standards. "It's as if they wanted the Constitution to matter only when it suited them," Leonard told me.

Adoption III

In 1997, Crooks moved again. Armed with the IBIA's reasoning that tribes had the right to interpret their own constitutions, he introduced Adoption Ordinance III. Once more, qualified members appealed to Washington. Once more, Assistant Secretary Kevin Gover allowed the ninety-day review window to expire without action, leaving the ordinance tacitly approved.

This inaction carried consequences far beyond Shakopee. Across Indian Country, Tribal leaders watched as the Department of the Interior in effect sanctioned membership expansion without constitutional amendment. Attorneys whispered of precedent—if Shakopee could do it, why not others?

Leonard traveled at his own expense to Washington, to universities, even abroad, arguing that Tribal citizenship was not a flexible commodity but the bedrock of sovereignty. He warned that allowing constitutions to be bent for short-term political advantage would corrode the very foundations of Tribal government.

NIGA and the Strain of Defense

Within the National Indian Gaming Association, the adoptee controversy strained credibility. Leonard and other officers spent hours explaining to congressional staff that IGRA did not authorize wholesale adoption of non-qualified members. Yet opponents of Indian gaming were quick to brandish Shakopee as proof that tribes could not police themselves.

State attorneys general seized the narrative in compact negotiations. "If Shakopee can simply add members," they argued, "then surely states should have a say in regulating Tribal enrollments as part of gaming oversight." It was a dangerous line—one that risked dragging states into the sacred realm of citizenship.

NIGA pushed back hard, reminding Congress that sovereignty meant tribes alone determined their members. But the fight was uphill. Each adoption ordinance in Shakopee became fodder for those who wanted to erode IGRA and tilt compacts in favor of the states.

A Shadow Over Sovereignty

By the late 1990s, the adoptee battles had become inseparable from the story of Indian gaming itself. Court cases piled up. Federal officials issued contradictory letters. The BIA alternated between disapprovals and silences. And all the while, money flowed—per capita payments, mortgages, land assignments—into the hands of people the Constitution had never recognized.

For Leonard, the irony was bitter. He had helped secure IGRA's passage, had fought for compacts that respected sovereignty in perpetuity, had even persuaded Congress to include video gaming in the federal framework. Yet back home, his own tribe was undermining those gains, proving to hostile governors and legislators that sovereignty could be twisted for profit.

The adoptee struggle did not end in the 1990s. It carried forward into the new millennium, a running sore that reopened with every election, every ordinance, every court appeal. For Shakopee, it was the defining internal conflict of its modern history. For Indian Country, it was a cautionary tale—an example of how fragile sovereignty could be when constitutions were ignored, and how quickly one tribe's turmoil could become every tribe's burden in the eyes of Congress and the states.

Into the New Millennium

The adoptee controversy did not fade with the close of the 1990s. If anything, it deepened. Every new ordinance, every BIA letter, every ruling or silence from Washington hardened the battle lines within Shakopee. Families grew further apart. Some spoke of betrayal, others of opportunity. What had once been a community of barely a hundred people living on dusty roads had become a multimillion-dollar economy where membership meant life-changing wealth.

And membership was precisely what the Constitution was meant to protect. The quarter-blood requirement and the link to the 1886 rolls were not arbitrary. They were the historical tether to those who had suffered through the aftermath of 1862. Yet in practice, Chairman Stan Crooks' adoption ordinances loosened that tether. People with no verifiable claim now stood shoulder to shoulder with descendants of the 1886 friendlies, voting in elections, drawing per capita checks, and receiving mortgages worth hundreds of thousands of dollars.

It was not only a legal rupture, it was a cultural one.

The Cost of Division

By the 2000s, Shakopee was no longer a struggling reservation. Mystic Lake had become one of the most successful Tribal casinos in the nation, generating hundreds of millions of dollars in revenue each year. With that success came per capita payments to members so large they drew headlines across the country.

Journalists, often unaware of the constitutional battles underneath, painted Shakopee as a tribe awash in wealth. Few reported on the fracture between qualified descendants and adoptees, or the lawsuits that had dragged through federal courts for years. To the public, it was a story of Indians who had finally "made it"—with little acknowledgment of the cost to historical integrity.

Inside the community, though, the wound remained open. Qualified members who had spent decades proving their lineage felt their voices diminishing. Adoptees, empowered by per capita distributions and by Crooks' political machine, consolidated influence. Elections turned not on debates about sovereignty or economic development, but on who could protect payouts.

Echoes Beyond Shakopee

The adoptee issue did not stay contained. Across Indian Country, other tribes that were watching Shakopee wrestled with the temptation to broaden membership rolls in order to share in gaming wealth. Some resisted, holding firmly to blood quantum and base rolls. Others experimented, opening the door to lineal descendants without regard to quantum, or passing ordinances of their own.

The result was uneven. In some tribes, it led to reconciliation and growth. In others, it ignited feuds as bitter as those in Shakopee.

For federal officials, it was chaos. The Bureau of Indian Affairs, long derelict in its fiduciary duty, now faced a flood of enrollment disputes. Courts grew weary of hearing cases that seemed never to end. And in Congress, every new adoption battle became another argument for more oversight, more regulation, more ways to chip away at sovereignty.

A Legacy Still Unsettled

By the 2010s, the adoptee issue was still unresolved. Ordinances stood on shaky ground, federal reviews had been inconsistent, and

Shakopee's reputation remained double-edged—admired for its wealth, questioned for its integrity.

Leonard, reflecting on the decades of struggle, had often put it simply: "If you don't know who your members are, how do you know who your leaders are? And if you don't know who your leaders are, how can the federal government claim to be working with a sovereign government at all?"

It was the question at the heart of the adoptee fight—a question that outlasted court rulings, ordinances, and even administrations.

And it was a question that, unanswered, cast a long shadow not only over Shakopee, but over every tribe whose sovereignty depended on the fragile promise of recognition.

An Act of God

Leonard had once remarked that only "an act of God" could undo the corporate protections of Little Six, Inc.—the firewall he had built to separate business from politics. In the end, that act of God was no lightning bolt from the sky, but a man—Stanley Crooks.

By dismantling Little Six, by fostering adoption ordinances, and by overseeing per capita distributions to those constitutionally unqualified, Crooks reshaped the community. By the end of his administration, the Mdewakanton community was wealthier than ever. but, in Leonard's eyes, it was also more divided, less lawful, and at risk of losing the very sovereignty that had made its success possible.

The Rise and Missteps of Foxwoods

Lessons Beyond Shakopee

By the early 1990s, it was tempting for critics of Indian gaming to treat Shakopee's disputes—membership battles, corporate dismantling, and political infighting—as though they were peculiar to one small Dakota community. They were not. The storm that came with gaming swept across Indian Country, bringing wealth, division, and temptation in equal measure.

And if anyone doubted that point, they had only to look eastward to the wooded hills of Connecticut. There, a tribe even smaller than Shakopee in population, but infinitely more ambitious in construction, had built the largest casino in the world. Foxwoods was meant to be the crown jewel of Indian gaming. Instead, it became a cautionary tale, a reminder that bigger was not always better and that sovereignty could be weakened as easily by overreach as by neglect.

The Mashantucket Pequots: A Small Nation, a Giant Dream

The Mashantucket Pequot Tribe had lived on a modest land base in southeastern Connecticut. Their numbers were tiny—fewer than sixty enrolled members at the moment Foxwoods opened its doors. Their landholdings were slightly larger than Shakopee's but still no match for the expanse of Las Vegas or Atlantic City.

Shakopee, by comparison, had around one hundred enrolled members at the same time, with just 250 acres of trust land. Two tribes, both small, both overlooked for generations—yet both destined to transform Indian gaming.

Where Mystic Lake began with a single 130,000-square-foot building—which grew to 360,000 square feet within a year—Foxwoods went straight to the stratosphere: over 340,000 square feet of gaming floor and eventually 4.7 million square feet of resort complex. What Shakopee built step by step, the Pequots attempted in a single leap.

Licensing: Contracts That Cost Sovereignty

Foxwoods' first great misstep was in its licensing and management agreements. Eager to project the aura of Las Vegas, the Pequots signed contracts that gave enormous leverage to outside corporations. Consultants and vendors from Nevada and New Jersey negotiated terms that siphoned off millions in fees and tied the tribe to long-term obligations. Even slot machine licensing came at higher costs, leaving the tribe with less control over its core asset.

Shakopee had taken a different approach. Their Bingo Lounge had already taught them the dangers of management contracts. Instead of surrendering control, Mystic Lake had purchased machines outright when possible. When leasing was necessary, they pressed vendors into competition—Novamatic versus Kiland, European suppliers versus domestic. Where Foxwoods paid inflated fees, they leveraged their sovereign position to drive them down.

The difference showed in the bottom line: Mystic Lake retained a greater percentage of its revenue, while Foxwoods' spectacular gross receipts were eaten alive by contractual obligations.

Overbuilding: Palaces in the Woods

Flush with cash in the first years, the Pequots expanded Foxwoods into a palace that rivaled anything on the Strip. Luxury hotels rose over the forest canopy. Shopping promenades and theaters multiplied. Debt piled as quickly as concrete. For a time, buses from Boston and New York filled the floors, but when the novelty waned and nearby competitors like Mohegan Sun opened, Foxwoods found itself saddled with billions in obligations.

Mystic Lake grew too—but on steadier legs. They added hotels, entertainment venues, and conference space gradually, each expansion financed by existing revenue rather than borrowed billions. Mystic Lake never reached Foxwoods' dazzling square footage, but it remained nimbler, more solvent, and ultimately more profitable on a per capita basis.

Governance and Accountability

At Shakopee, governance was messy, loud, and often bitter. Factions argued in parking lots. Membership battles spilled into courtrooms. But those very conflicts forced their community to wrestle with the Constitution and to defend the principle that sovereignty meant rules applied to everyone.

At Foxwoods, decision-making was concentrated in a handful of leaders. With so few Tribal citizens, accountability mechanisms were thin. Strategic errors—like overbuilding or bad licensing—went largely unchallenged until they had already set like concrete.

By the late 1990s, as Foxwoods began restructuring its debts, reports circulated that, on a per-member basis, Shakopee's distributions outpaced those of the Pequots. The irony was rich: The "world's largest casino" was less profitable for its People than the "little bingo tribe" from Minnesota.

A National Cautionary Tale

Foxwoods dazzled outsiders. The press wrote endlessly about the "richest Indians in America." Senators and governors toured the halls. But beneath the lights, sovereignty was quietly compromised. Outsider contracts drained profits. Overbuilding chained the tribe to Wall Street bankers. Governance faltered under the weight of secrecy and debt.

By comparison, Mystic Lake's story—troubled as it was—looked almost prudent. Its problems were real: adoptees, per capita disputes, dismantled corporations. But its financial model was sounder, its growth steadier, its sovereignty more intact.

Foxwoods became the larger cautionary tale—proof that size does not guarantee success and that sovereignty without discipline can collapse under its own weight.

The Broader Lesson

The story of Foxwoods did not erase the story of Shakopee; it sharpened it. Mystic Lake's critics at home saw dysfunction, but national leaders saw something else... a tribe stayed solvent while a giant stumbled.

The lesson for Indian Country was clear. Sovereignty is not only the right to build—it is the responsibility to build wisely. It requires discipline, foresight, and respect for constitutional governance. Without those, even the largest casino in the world can falter.

Foxwoods remains a landmark, its towers still gleaming over the Connecticut woods. But its legacy is as much a warning as a triumph. For Shakopee, and for all of Indian Country, the message was simple: Measure your growth by wisdom, not just by square footage.

Diverging Paths

By the early 2000s, the cracks in Foxwoods' empire could no longer be papered over. Debt from its vast expansion projects had mounted into the billions. Wall Street creditors—never sentimental about sovereignty—demanded repayment schedules and refinancing terms that left the Pequots scrambling to protect their core assets. Headlines about restructuring replaced the earlier triumphal narratives about the "world's largest casino."

At the same moment, Mystic Lake was walking a very different road. Their revenues, though modest compared to Foxwoods' gross take, were steady, reliable, and free of crushing debt service. They invested cautiously in hotels, event centers, and conference facilities. They gave millions in charitable contributions to Minnesota towns, schools, and hospitals. Politicians who once dismissed Shakopee as "just another bingo hall" now came courting, recognizing their tribe as a steady partner in regional development.

Foxwoods' stumble, paired with Mystic Lake's stability, flipped the script. The massive Connecticut project was forced into negotiations with outside financiers, while the little Dakota community in Minnesota strengthened its political and charitable presence. One tribe carried the weight of overreach; the other, despite its internal turmoil, carried the proof that sovereignty and prudence could coexist.

The contrast was not lost on Indian Country. Leaders across the Nation spoke quietly of the lesson: The size of a building or the flash of a headline does not define success. What defines it is the ability to control your own affairs, resist predatory contracts, and grow at a pace your People can sustain.

For Shakopee, the juxtaposition was vindication. For Foxwoods, it was a warning echoed in every Tribal council chamber that dared to dream too quickly.

The Echo of Little Crow

History has a way of circling back on itself. Sometimes the arc is visible, like a river looping through the same low ground. Sometimes it runs unseen, an underground current pushing the present toward the shape of the past. For Leonard Prescott, leader of the Shakopee Mdewakanton Sioux Community in one of its most turbulent and transformative eras, that current was embodied in the figure of Taoyateduta—known to the world as Little Crow.

The Shadow of 1862

Every Dakota child grows up in the shadow of 1862. The war, the uprising, the gallows at Mankato—it is the crucible in which identity is forged. For Leonard, born into a family where survival meant moving between the margins of city and reservation, those events were not just history lessons; they were reminders of dispossession still felt in housing, in work, and in the very question of who counted as a member of the community.

Little Crow, in 1862, faced impossible choices. Trapped between promises broken by the federal government and the hunger of his People, he was thrust into a role he did not seek. Accounts of the time show him as reluctant, almost resigned, to lead his warriors into a fight he knew could not be won. Yet when the general council of Dakota men pressed him—when the weight of his People's despair left him no option—he stepped forward, calm, deliberate, and willing to bear the burden of consequence.

Leonard, more than a century later, echoed that same reluctant assumption of power. He never campaigned for glory, never sought to be "the man in charge." By his own admission, he once thought he would spend his life bending sheet metal and punching union cards. Yet when the petition to remove Chairman Norm Crooks reached a breaking point, it was Leonard who was called forward. When the papers of removal had to be delivered, it was Leonard who carried them across the floor of the council hall. Like Little Crow, he did not go forward in triumph but in necessity.

Calm Amid Faction

Little Crow was remembered—even by his enemies—for a peculiar calmness. He was not a man of bluster. He did not roar or pound the drum of war in reckless fury. He spoke carefully, often pausing before answering, weighing words with the same gravity as he weighed decisions. That composure was mistaken by some for indecision. In reality, it was the deep patience of a man who understood that choices made in haste could cost lives and futures.

Leonard mirrored that temperament. In council meetings wracked by factional shouting, where family lines divided the room and tempers sparked into physical confrontations in parking lots, he held his voice steady. He listened longer than he spoke. He took the time to walk house to house, explaining compacts, ordinances, and enrollment rules—not because it was efficient, but because it was just. Like Little Crow, he carried a burden heavier than the words he spoke. Calmness was not weakness. It was strength in a storm.

The Weight of Betrayal

Little Crow's legacy was scarred by betrayal. Federal agents who promised food withheld it. Traders who extended credit cut the Dakota People off at the moment of deepest hunger. When he finally took up arms, it was less an act of ambition than an act of survival. Yet when the war ended, it was his body that was desecrated, his scalp displayed in ridicule in Minnesota's halls of government.

Leonard, too, carried the weight of betrayal. He had built Mystic Lake and Little Six Inc. only to see the structures dismantled by political adversaries and opportunists. He worked to secure constitutional integrity in membership, only to see it subverted by adoption ordinances. He defended the sovereignty of his People in Washington, only to be dragged through decades of lawsuits in his own community's courts. Like Little Crow, he knew what it was to have labors undone, achievements twisted, and enemies made not by choice but by duty.

And yet—just as Little Crow's image has slowly shifted from vilification to recognition—Leonard's legacy, even if contested in his lifetime, stands as a testimony to vision, perseverance, and integrity.

Parallel Lives, Divergent Eras

It is tempting to press the comparison too far. Little Crow lived in a century when Native survival meant resisting outright extermination. Leonard lived in an era when survival meant navigating sovereignty within a legal and economic system designed by others. One carried a rifle into battle; the other carried documents into courtrooms and lobbied senators in marble corridors. Yet the parallels remain striking.

Both were reluctant leaders.

Both sought compromise before confrontation.

Both carried their People's divisions on their shoulders.

Both were betrayed by the systems that claimed to recognize them. Both endured the loneliness of leadership.

The Quiet Admiration

Leonard rarely said so openly, but those who knew him sensed a quiet admiration for Little Crow. Perhaps it was subconscious, a reflection of inherited memory rather than explicit study. Or perhaps, in long nights of reflection, Leonard considered what it meant to be a leader when leadership came not by desire but by necessity. The calmness. The gravity. The willingness to be misunderstood for the sake of the People.

When Leonard defended the integrity of the 1886 rolls, when he pushed for compacts that would last not just for a term but for generations, when he resisted the temptation to cash out sovereignty for quick profits, he was—whether consciously or not—walking in the path Little Crow had cleared through fire.

Coda: The Burden and the Gift

Every leader leaves a paradox. Little Crow was condemned in his day, yet honored in memory. Leonard endured hostility in his time, yet left institutions and precedents that others now take for granted. Both men bore the truth that leadership is less about triumph than endurance—less about the applause of the moment than the judgment of history.

For Leonard, the mirror of Little Crow was not perfect but profound. Both men remind us that sovereignty is never secure, that leadership demands sacrifice, and that calmness in the storm is not passivity but courage.

And here, at the book's end, the circle closes with the story we began with—the prophecy of the New Buffalo. This vision promised that survival would not come from grassland herds alone, but from a

Buffalo born of two worlds, carrying the strength of tradition and the tools of modernity. That Buffalo became Tribal gaming, the unlikely beast that fed and clothed Indian Country in the late twentieth century.

Leonard Prescott understood, as Little Crow once did, that survival requires transformation. The buffalo no longer thunders across the plains, but the spirit of renewal can still be captured if one has the patience, the courage, and the vision to see it. Leonard's life, with all its trials and betrayals, is bound to that prophecy. In him, the reluctant hunter donned the strange garments of another world—suits, ties, legal briefs—and walked into marble corridors, not to abandon tradition but to claim the New Buffalo for his People.

That is his legacy—like Little Crow, he bears the burden of divided loyalties and impossible choices. But unlike Little Crow, he has lived to see a prophecy fulfilled, to taste the first fruits of sovereignty reborn. The New Buffalo stands now on Dakota land, proof that sacrifice and leadership can, across generations, carry a People from hunger to hope, from weakness to strength, from dreams to reality.

Acknowledgements

I am deeply indebted to the following individuals, without whom this book could not have been created and published: Rick Polad, my stalwart and genius copyeditor who corrected and perfected my prose for clarity and accuracy; Ian Graham Leask, my publisher at Calumet Editions; and Joshua Weber, director of operations at Calumet. I also give special thanks to Pablo Murillo for helping to bring this project to fruition.

For all of us, this book has been an eye opener, and has helped us appreciate the enormous capacity of humans to perform tasks of great injustice as well as self-sacrifice for the greater good. My appreciaton also goes out to Leonard Prescott for his cooperation in the telling of this story.

About the Author

Before starting his career in writing and publishing books, Gary Lindberg was an award-winning filmmaker with over a hundred national and international awards. He produced and co-wrote the Paramount feature film *That Was Then, This Is Now* starring Emilio Estevez and Morgan Freeman. Since then, he has authored four #1 bestselling novels and many nonfiction titles. He lives in Minnesota where he has published books for over 150 authors with his partner at Calumet Editions, Ian Graham Leask.

www.ingramcontent.com/pod-product-compliance
Lightning Source LLC
LaVergne TN
LVHW091117080826
845145LV00008B/1955
9781962834636